DATE DUE

BRODART   Cat. No. 23-221

Revolutions
and
Revolutionary Waves

Revolutions
and
Revolutionary Waves

Mark N. Katz

St. Martin's Press
New York

ISBN 0-312-17322-9

Library of Congress Cataloging-in-Publication Data

Katz, Mark N.
    Revolutions and revolutionary waves / Mark N. Katz.
        p.   cm.
    Includes bibliographical references (p.   ) and index.
    ISBN 0-312-17322-9
    1. Revolutions. I. Title.
    JC491.K286 1997
    303.6'4—dc21   97-11237
                                                            CIP

Design by The Tern Book Company, Inc.

First edition: August, 1997
10 9 8 7 6 5 4 3 2 1

To Melissa

Contents

Acknowledgements

A generous grant from the United States Institute of Peace for the 1994-95 academic year allowed me the freedom to undertake the research and much of the writing for this study. I am especially grateful to Chester A. Crocker, the chairman of the Institute's board of trustees, for his support for this project.

Additional aid was received from the George Mason University International Institute. Thanks are due both to John Moore, the Institute's initial director, and to Louise White, his successor, for their sponsorship of my research. An award from the National Endowment for the Humanities to participate in its 1995 summer seminar on "Re-Imagining Societies: The Middle East and Central Asia" at Dartmouth College provided me with the opportunity to continue the writing in an idyllic setting. Dale F. Eickelman ably directed the seminar, creating a stimulating and hospitable environment in which all the participants could pursue their work and share ideas with one another.

I am deeply indebted to Adeed Dawisha of George Mason University, Torbjorn L. Knutsen of the University of Trondheim, Cynthia McClintock of George Washington University, and Robert W. Tucker, formerly of the Johns Hopkins University School of Advanced International Studies (SAIS), for having read and commented on the manuscript. Special thanks are due to Ilya Prizel of Johns Hopkins SAIS and Karen Wolny of St. Martin's Press. I would also like to thank Marjorie Gentry of Riverside, California, for her service as my volunteer research assistant. My wife, Nancy V. Yinger, strongly encouraged me to undertake this project and provided enthusiastic support throughout all phases of it.

This book is dedicated to our daughter, Melissa Yinger Katz, who since her birth in 1993 has worked a joyous revolution in our lives.

Preface

Revolutions upset the existing international order. But not all revolutions upset it equally. Revolutionary regimes that attempt to export their revolution by force of arms are especially frightening to the status quo powers. Although accommodation may be attempted for a while, the status quo powers usually see their interests as being so threatened that they either undertake a large-scale effort to roll back this type of expansion militarily or, at minimum, mobilize a military alliance to prevent it from expanding further.

But the type of revolution that is most disruptive to the existing international order is that which spreads (or credibly threatens to spread) not through invasion, but through one revolution's sparking affiliate revolutions elsewhere. In other words, what is disruptive is not just that an ideological revolutionary regime seeks the establishment of regimes similar to itself elsewhere, but that the revolutionary idea resonates in other countries, and significant forces appear that seek to implement it. For the status quo powers, containing a revolution from spreading via affiliate revolutions can be far more complex than rolling back or containing a revolution that spreads via invasion. For in the former case, it is not sufficient to militarily confront or contain the country in which the revolution initially succeeded. In addition, indigenous revolutionary forces must either be stopped from gaining strength in other countries, or successfully suppressed if they do. The history of the latter half of the twentieth century has shown, however, that the attempt to suppress indigenous revolutionary forces can be extremely difficult—indeed, can fail completely in some countries and thus lead to an even greater revolutionary challenge to the interests of the status quo powers.

While the policy of containment pursued by the United States and its West European allies must be judged a success in terms of deterring a Soviet invasion of Western Europe, it proved woefully inadequate in preventing Marxist-Leninist revolutionaries in Asia, Africa, and Latin America from coming to power and maintaining alliances with Moscow. Similarly, the West was unable to contain Arab nationalist revolutionaries who were inspired by the example of Egypt's Jamal 'Abd al-Nasir from seizing power in several other Arab countries. At present, the United States, Western Europe, and Russia are fearful of the wave of Islamic fundamentalist revolutions that swept to power in Iran, Sudan, and Afghanistan, and that threatens to spread to Algeria, Egypt, and other countries in the Middle East, Central Asia, and elsewhere in the Muslim world.

From the perspective of the mid-1990s, the wave of Islamic fundamentalist revolutions seems to be increasing ominously whereas both the Marxist-Leninist and Arab nationalist revolutionary waves appear to be spent forces. This is especially true of the Marxist-Leninist revolutionary wave after the downfall of communism in Eastern Europe in 1989 and the breakup of the Soviet Union in 1991. Most of the Marxist-Leninist regimes of the Third World have also been transformed, and those few that have not are devoting their energy to staying in power and competing with other countries for Western investment instead of trying to foment revolution elsewhere. The Arab nationalist regimes, far from being part of a self-confident revolutionary movement that other Arabs see as a model, have increasingly found themselves on the defensive against Islamic fundamentalist revolutionaries.

Will the Islamic fundamentalist revolutionary wave eventually dissipate as have the Marxist-Leninist and Arab nationalist waves? It is my contention that nondemocratic revolutionary waves that spread via affiliate revolutions experience their own unique pattern of expansion, affiliation and disaffiliation, and then collapse.

It may be objected that there are so many important differences among Marxist-Leninist, Arab nationalist, and Islamic fundamentalist revolutions that they cannot be directly compared with one another. I readily acknowledge that there are such differences. I do not seek to reshape the histories of these revolutions so that they can be easily "explained" by a theory about their similarities. But just as there are important differences among these three revolutionary waves, there are also important differences within them. Besides, the issue to be examined here is not what conditions give rise to different types of revolution or why certain types of revolution succeed in some countries but not in others. The analysis focuses instead on why revolutionary movements and regimes in different countries choose to affiliate or disaffiliate with one another. Despite the many differences in their origins, ideologies, international relations and other factors, I will argue here that common patterns are observable in the relations among revolutions within these three revolutionary waves.

A more important objection is that since these three revolutionary waves are at different stages of the life cycle I have referred to, they cannot be readily compared. Specifically, just because the Marxist-Leninist and Arab nationalist waves have (in very different ways from each other) collapsed, there is no necessity that the Islamic fundamentalist wave—which is still expanding—will also collapse. It is not my purpose to predict exactly how far the Islamic fundamentalist revolutionary wave will expand or at what point it will begin to recede. What I seek to do instead is argue that the Islamic fundamentalist revolutionary wave, like the Marxist-Leninist and Arab nationalist waves, belongs to a category of nondemocratic revolutions that spread via affiliate revolutions, and thus it may more readily be understood in terms of this pattern than some other one, such as nondemocratic revolutions that spread via invasion. This is an especially important point to grasp in terms of the formulation of policy by status quo governments in response to revolutionary waves. Policies that are effective in containing revolutions that spread via invasion have often proven counterproductive when they are applied to revolutions that spread via affiliate revolutions. Furthermore, I hope to show that, despite its actual successes and seemingly impending successes elsewhere, the Islamic fundamentalist revolutionary wave is subject to the same problems and internal contradictions that contributed to the collapse of the Marxist-Leninist and Arab nationalist revolutionary waves.

Revolutions
and
Revolutionary Waves

Chapter 1

Revolutions and Revolutionary Waves

The object of this study is to understand how revolutionaries espousing the same ideology or similar ones relate to one another as well as to the status quo, nonrevolutionary powers in the international system. It will be argued here that indigenous Marxist-Leninist, Arab nationalist, and Islamic fundamentalist revolutions are each examples of a specific type of revolutionary wave (which I describe as nondemocratic "for" waves that expand primarily via affiliate revolution) and thus have a similar pattern of expansion, affiliation and disaffiliation, before collapsing. Chapters 2 through 4 will analyze each of these phases in this particular type of revolutionary wave. Before this, however, the concept of revolutionary waves in general will be examined in this chapter. First, though, something must be said about the units that comprise revolutionary waves: individual revolutions.

There is an enormous literature on revolution. Much of it discusses why revolution occurs. Not surprisingly, no general consensus has been reached on this question; there are many competing explanations.[1] It is not my purpose to review this vast literature on why revolution occurs but to discuss the three aspects of individual revolutions that are necessary for understanding revolutionary waves: 1) how revolutions occur, 2) what revolutions accomplish, and 3) the roles that individual revolutions may play in a larger revolutionary wave. First, however, some attention must be paid to definitional issues concerning revolution.

REVOLUTION: COMPETING DEFINITIONS

In his classic study on revolutions, Crane Brinton noted that the term "revolution" means different things to different people. He defined revolution as the "drastic, sudden substitution of one group in charge of the running of a territorial political entity by another group hitherto not running that government" (1965, 4). For Brinton and others, though, the fact that such a drastic change occurs is not sufficient to define a revolution: *how* this drastic change occurs has been the crucial factor for many scholars in determining whether a "drastic change" in government is a revolution or not.

Brinton believed that a revolution could occur by several means, including violent uprising, coup d'etat, "or some other kind of skullduggery"; he did not, however, think that a revolution could be made without violence (1965, 4). But even with this limitation, a wide variety of phenomena could be classified as revolution in accordance with Brinton's definition. Theda Skocpol, by contrast, employs a much narrower definition of revolution. For her, the true revolution is a social revolution involving "rapid, basic transformations of a society's state and class structures" (1979, 4). For Skocpol, social revolution transforms both the political and the social structure of a nation and occurs through "intense sociopolitical conflicts in which class struggles play a key role" (1979, 5). Because she envisioned social revolution only as a cathartic class struggle, it is not surprising that Skocpol concluded that "social revolutions have been rare" (1979, 1); for her, the establishment of a new regime by other means does not constitute a revolution. Fifteen years after the publication of her seminal book, *States and Social Revolutions,* she continued to maintain that ever since the French Revolution, the only successful revolutions have been peasant revolutions—the Iranian Revolution of 1978-79 being the sole exception (1994, 16).

The problem with Skocpol's definition is that it only recognizes successful peasant rebellion as resulting in revolution. Even Brinton's broader definition of revolution would not include the upheavals that overthrew the Communist regimes in Poland, Czechoslovakia, Hungary, Bulgaria, and East Germany in 1989—because they were largely peaceful. Yet these were arguably social revolutions in the Skocpolian sense in that they involved the transformation of both political and social structures in these states.

More importantly for the purposes of this study, a narrow definition of revolution, based on the insistence that it can only occur in a certain way, does not reflect the practice of revolutionaries themselves. Skocpol notwithstanding, many regimes that have come to power as a result of a coup d'etat instead of a protracted guerrilla struggle have not felt in the least constrained or embarrassed about declaring themselves to be revolutionary. Further, such regimes have often been accepted as revolutionary by other revolutionary regimes that came to power via guerrilla struggle.

In determining whether a given regime is revolutionary, attention must be paid to whether it declares itself to be so as well as whether other governments, especially other revolutionary ones, acknowledge its revolutionary nature. Still, too much emphasis must not be placed on self-definition or recognition by other governments as forms of definition. Self-definition alone cannot always be relied upon: it is possible that a regime may declare itself to be revolutionary when it is not in order to obtain support or avoid being the target of powerful revolutionary states. And as Henry Munson has pointed out, those who stage a coup d'etat are usually inclined to refer to what they have done as a revolution whether it actually is one or not (1988, viii). In addition, revolutionary regimes have often denounced one another as unrevolutionary even though they may previously have proclaimed themselves to be in unshakable revolutionary solidarity. Finally, the designation of a regime to be revolutionary by a status quo government may reflect more the latter's fears than the former's reality. Just as too narrow a definition of revolution can exclude actual revolutions from consideration, too broad a definition risks identifying as revolutions phenomena or events that are not. While scholars may be more prone to the former error, policymakers are more susceptible to the latter one.

According to Forrest Colburn, "revolution is the sudden, violent, and drastic substitution of one group governing a territorial political entity for another group formerly excluded from the government, *and* an ensuing assault on state and society for the purpose of radically transforming society" (1994, 6). This insistence that revolution occur violently appears especially unnecessary considering that since 1989 several East European governments that came to power more or less peacefully have been more successful at "radically transforming society" than have many other revolutionary regimes that came to power violently. But except for this caveat, Colburn's definition of revolution is useful since it focuses more on what a revolutionary regime accomplishes (or sets out to accomplish) than on how it came to power. Indeed, Colburn argues that "it does not matter how, or even why" they occur (1994, 7).

Yet if the means by which a revolution takes place is not necessarily related to its accomplishments, how a revolution occurs can be important for understanding the resulting regime's strengths and weaknesses as well as its relations with both other revolutionary regimes and with status quo governments.

How Revolutions Occur

Historically, there have been five kinds of revolution: 1) rural revolution; 2) urban revolution; 3) coup d'état; 4) revolution "from above;" and 5) revolution "from without."

Rural revolution usually involves the successful organization of the peasantry into a guerrilla army that fights an insurgency. As noted earlier, Skocpol saw rural revolution as the only successful type occurring anywhere (except Iran) during the past two hundred years. This kind of revolution can involve a protracted conflict during which the revolutionary forces gain control over a significant portion of the countryside, and then sweep dramatically into the capital after the forces fighting to protect the status quo have been defeated, withdrawn, or demoralized.

Sometimes rural revolution is referred to as "peasant revolution," but this is a misnomer. As Leonard Binder pointed out, those who have made revolution in the name of the peasantry have moved to suppress it once they have come to power (1988, 62-74).[2]

Rural revolution in the twentieth century is usually associated with Marxist-Leninist revolution, but this has not always been true. Olivier Roy described the overthrow of the Marxist-Leninist regime in Afghanistan in 1992 as the culmination of a successful rural revolution waged by Islamic fundamentalist revolutionary forces in that country (1994, 50).

Urban revolution, by its very nature, occurs in a much more narrowly defined space than rural revolution. Unlike rural revolutionaries, who benefit from weak government control over remote areas in the countryside, urban revolutionaries usually do not have the ability to build up a powerful guerrilla army. Yet despite the superior military force that a government can more easily bring to bear in urban than in rural areas, Brinton observed that urban revolutionaries can still succeed through subversion of the government's armed forces (1965, 88). If this occurs, urban revolution may take place as the result of a general strike involving little or no fighting. In her comparative analysis of the Iranian and Nicaraguan Revolutions of 1979, Faridch Farhi noted the importance of the urban general strike in both cases (1990, 6). Some degree of violence, however, was involved in these two instances—especially in Nicaragua. But the general strike succeeded in an almost purely nonviolent form in the capitals of several East European nations in 1989 and in Moscow in 1991.

While Skocpol saw Iran's successful 1979 urban revolution as an exception, one of her critics described it as the beginning of a trend (Ahmad 1982, 293-94). Although it was rural in Afghanistan, Islamic fundamentalist revolution is generally an urban phenomenon in the Middle East (Ayubi 1991, 226; Roy 1994, 50). This may have highly significant future consequences. For as Jeffrey Simon has observed, while rural revolution may take years or even decades to succeed, in urban revolutions, "Governments can be toppled in a matter of weeks, and countries can become paralyzed overnight" (1989, 5).

Even more than urban revolutions, coups d'état can take place with little or no warning. Of course, a successful coup d'état does not always—or even usually—equal a revolution, especially if the coup simply leads to one group of military officers replacing another. Nor can most of those instances in which coups d'état overthrew democratic governments, such as those that occurred in Latin America, be considered revolutions either. While suppressing democracy, the coup leaders in these cases usually did not launch a general assault to reshape society as a whole.

Some coups d'état, however, must be considered as revolutions since a new leadership not only emerged but set about radically restructuring society. One of the most important coups d'état that led to revolutionary change occurred in Egypt in 1952. Jamal 'Abd al-Nasir and his colleagues were not satisfied to simply oust King Farouk and rule over Egyptian society as it was; they set out to remake society completely according to their notions of "Arab nationalism" and "Arab socialism." Their efforts captured the imagination of not only the Egyptian public, but of the Arab world as a whole. The 1952 Free Officers' coup did not lead just to a revolution, but to the initiation of a powerful revolutionary wave throughout the Arab world.

While a coup d'état may lead to dramatic change in the top political leadership but little or no change in the social structure, a revolution "from above" can lead to the opposite. In a revolution from above, it is the existing political leadership (or part of it) which undertakes the rapid transformation of society by coercive means. The existing political leadership can also transform the government bureaucracy as a whole in this type of revolution.

Revolutions from above can be divided into two categories: accelerative and preemptive. An accelerative revolution from above is one in which a revolutionary regime already in power launches the ambitious social engineering projects that it had in mind when it first seized power but was unable to implement. Examples of accelerative revolutions from above include Stalin's First Five Year Plan in the USSR (1928-32) and Mao's Great Leap Forward in China (1958).

A preemptive revolution from above, by contrast, involves an effort by a regime to implement the program of an increasingly popular revolutionary ideology in order to prevent revolutionaries from ousting the regime. An example of a preemptive revolution from above occurred in Sudan in 1983, when Jaafar al-Numayri, who had come to power as the leader of an Arab nationalist revolution in 1969, tried to undercut the appeal of Islamic opposition groups by introducing the *sharia* himself. Al-Numayri's government was overthrown in 1985, but the *sharia* laws he introduced have remained in effect ever since (Warburg 1990).

A fifth type of revolution is what I call revolution "from without." This occurs when one country invades another and then proceeds to reorganize the latter's government and society in a manner similar to its own. Examples of this include revolutions brought to East Germany, Poland, Hungary, Romania, Bulgaria, and North Korea by the Soviet Union at the end of World War II. Revolution from without also occurred in West Germany, Italy, and Japan at this time, though in these cases it came primarily from the United States.

Most students of revolution do not consider revolutions from without since they do not result primarily from internal forces as do other types of revolution. But while a revolution from without is obviously imposed upon a nation that experiences it, many internally based revolutions—especially coups d'etat—are brought about by a tiny minority. In neither case is the development or longevity of a revolutionary regime dependent on popular support. Further, even though a revolution may be imposed by one nation on another, an externally imposed revolutionary regime can take root within the nation that experienced it. The democratic revolution that the United States and its allies imposed on West Germany, for example, developed strong roots; despite the dramatic headlines, antidemocratic parties have not made a strong showing in West German—or, since 1990, united German—elections. The United States worked to install a system in which the Japanese Liberal Democratic party succeeded in monopolizing power for decades. This system of one-party "democracy" survived and took on a life of its own for many years after the decline of active American efforts to prop it up.[3]

An indication of the degree to which Marxist-Leninist revolutions from without took root in states bordering the former USSR has been the strength of former Communist parties in several East European nations where elections have been relatively free. Another such indication is the durability of the unreformed communist regime in North Korea, as well as the largely authoritarian regimes run by ex-communists in several of the republics of the former USSR.

Some Islamic fundamentalist groups—the so-called neofundamentalists—have adopted a sixth revolutionary strategy, which may be called revolution "by osmosis." Instead of seeking to seize power directly, neofundamentalist groups are attempting to slowly take control of the institutions of both society and government via the Islamization of individuals within them (Roy 1994, 79; Wickham 1994). If this process succeeds, however, it should probably not be termed revolution. As with the peaceful transfer of power in established democracy via elections, this type of change would be evolutionary and would not be the "sudden, drastic" change that is an integral part of revolution. Of course, if this gradual Islamization reaches a critical mass within a state, or in its military, a showdown with the government might occur. But this would then be some other form of revolution, such as urban revolution or coup d'etat. It must be emphasized, though, that the gradualist approach of the neofundamentalists has not yet succeeded in absorbing a government anywhere. Nor do targeted Arab governments appear willing to be absorbed in this manner, as the 1994-95 Egyptian government crackdown on the neofundamentalist Muslim Brotherhood demonstrated.[4]

Scholars often disagree over which cases should be considered examples of revolution. Yet even when there is general agreement that a revolution did take place in a specific country, there is often disagreement as to what type of revolution it should be considered. As was mentioned before, Skocpol maintained that *all* successful social revolutions except Iran's (1979) have involved rural revolution (1994, 16). By contrast, the revolutions in Russia (1917) and Nicaragua (1979) were described as being primarily urban by McDaniel (1991, 111-14) and Farhi (1990, 6-7), respectively. In fact, revolutions can and often do involve more than one of these methods, as the Russian, Chinese, and Sudanese cases show.

The Russian Revolution began with an urban revolution against the tsarist regime in February 1917. This was soon followed by autonomous rural uprisings elsewhere in the country. The coming-to-power of the Bolsheviks in November, however, was the result of a successful coup d'etat. After the civil war, the Thermidorean New Economic Policy (1922-28) was implemented while a power struggle within the Communist party took place, and the peasantry was allowed to keep the land it had seized during the rural uprisings. After defeating his rivals and obtaining complete autocratic power in 1928, Stalin launched a revolution from above, ending the relative independence that the peasants had earlier won and that the regime had up to then grudgingly respected. Gorbachev's perestroika can be considered an attempted revolution from above which he lost control over and which culminated in the urban revolution of August 1991 that led to the breakup of the USSR four months later.

After its failed urban uprisings in the 1920s, the Chinese Communist party came to power as a result of a rural revolution that culminated in 1949 when it successfully organized the peasantry into a guerrilla army. In 1958, Mao Tse-tung launched a revolution from above in which he asserted the party's authority over the peasantry. Despite its chaotic nature, the Cultural Revolution of 1966-69 can be seen as another revolution from above organized by Mao to reassert his authority over the party and state bureaucracy. After Mao's death in 1976, Deng Xiao-peng launched yet another revolution from above in order to bring about the capitalist transformation of China's economy. The Tiananmen massacre of 1989 was the suppression of an urban revolution against the regime.

The Islamic revolution in Sudan began with a revolution from above on the part of the hitherto Arab nationalist regime that introduced *sharia* law in 1983. This regime, however, succumbed to an urban revolution in 1985. Elections were held subsequently and resulted in the Islamic democrat, Sadiq al-Mahdi, becoming prime minister. The democratic government, however, was overthrown in 1989 through a coup d'etat involving the Islamized military as well as al-Mahdi's undemocratic, Islamic fundamentalist rival, Dr. Hasan Turabi. This Islamic fundamentalist regime that came to power in 1989 has not only sought to impose the *sharia* by force in the non-Islamic southern part of Sudan, but has provided support to a number of groups attempting to bring about Islamic fundamentalist revolution in several other countries.

The course of revolution in all countries could be schematized in this manner. Although many have followed similar paths (such as the revolutions from without at the end of World War II that occurred in several East European countries), there has been great variety in the mixture of methods by which revolution has occurred in those countries that have experienced it. Further, the course of the revolution does not necessarily cease with the overthrow of the old regime; as the three cases cited here show, revolutions are often protracted processes by which societies can experience repeated "drastic, sudden" changes.

REVOLUTIONARY OBJECTIVES

Just as revolutions occur by differing means, they also have differing objectives. Basically, though, every revolution has two sets of objectives: to rapidly get rid of whatever political or economic system the aspiring revolutionaries object to, and to replace it with an alternate system that they believe to be superior. In other words, a revolution is both against something and for something. But there is a wide variety of things that revolutions have opposed and promoted.

What Revolutions Are Against

In her book *Nationalism: Five Roads to Modernity,* Liah Greenfeld noted the centrality of what she termed *ressentiment* (resentment) in the emergence of nationalism (1992, 11). This feeling arises when people in one nation (or more accurately, intellectually and politically important people within that nation) envy the superior status of one or more other nations compared to their own, consider this state of affairs to be unjust, but are unable to rectify it, at least in the short run.

In my view, revolution occurs when this resentment (*resentment* being a perfectly serviceable word in English, it will be employed here instead of *ressentiment*) boils over and the revolutionaries seizing power attempt to rectify the situation all at once. But whereas the resentment of nationalists is directed against other nations, the resentment of revolutionaries can be directed against internal as well as external opponents. In the minds of the revolutionaries, however, this might not be an important distinction; as Brinton pointed out, revolutionaries often regard the hated regime they seek to oust as having been imposed by foreigners (1965, 48-49).

There has been a wide variety of opponents against which revolutions have been fought. Absolute monarchies have been the target of a number of revolutions, from the English Revolution of the seventeenth century to, most recently, the Iranian Revolution in the late twentieth century. There have also been a number of antidictatorial revolutions. A subset of antidictatorial revolutions are antirevolutionary revolutions: in other words, revolutions against regimes that originally came to power via revolutions themselves. These include the anticommunist revolutions in Eastern Europe in 1989 and Russia in 1991. Nazih Ayubi has pointed out that Islamic fundamentalist revolutionary movements in the Arab world are strongest in those countries that previously experienced Arab nationalist revolution (1991, 118-19). There have also been antidemocratic revolutions, such as the Nazi revolution in Germany and the falangist revolution in Spain in the 1930s.

Of course, it may not be just a regime that revolutionaries identify as their internal opponent; they may also seek to destroy the existing socioeconomic system. A number of revolutions have been fought against the "society of orders" dominated by an aristocracy determined largely by birth. There have also been a number of "anticapitalist" revolutions, though these have only occurred, paradoxically, in societies where capitalism was poorly developed. Islamic fundamentalist revolutionaries in Iran and elsewhere have not just been opposed to the regime in power, but to all aspects of their societies that they deem to be "un-Islamic."

Revolutions have also been fought against external opponents. The most common of these in the twentieth century have been anticolonial revolutions. In addition, dictatorial regimes supported by a foreign power have not only aroused revolutionary resentment against the regime itself, but also against its external supporters. The revolutions against the Shah of Iran and the Nicaraguan dictator Somoza had an anti-American character just as the revolution against the Marxist regime in Afghanistan was anti-Soviet. A revolution, then, can not only be fought against a regime, but also against a nation's place in the existing international order. Such a revolution can culminate in not only a "drastic, sudden" change in regime, but also in a similar change in that nation's alliances.

What Revolutions Are For

What a particular revolution is "for" does not always emerge as quickly as what it is "against." This is because its purpose is not as readily agreed upon among the revolutionaries. Colburn noted this phenomenon when he wrote, "In the poor countries of the world, revolutions have been fought (and won) not to build socialism or some other idealized society, but to dispose of colonialists or a despot" (1994, 64). While a successful revolution quickly dispenses with whatever it is against, what precisely it is for may be vigorously contested among the victorious revolutionaries who turn against one another after the object of their previous alliance—the old regime or colonial rule—has been eliminated. Even when there is general agreement among the revolutionaries as to their goal—be this democracy, socialism, or Islamic government—they may not agree on the exact form it should take. Indeed, there may be a transitional period lasting years before the precise goal is fully defined, as proved to be the case with socialism in the Soviet Union and Islamic government in Iran.

There have been a variety of purposes for which revolutions have been fought, including democracy and different nondemocratic systems of government (all of which described themselves as democratic), including fascism, Marxism-Leninism, Arab nationalism, Islamic fundamentalism, and others.

An important distinction between revolutions is that some have relatively limited or unambitious aims whereas others have more ambitious ones. An unambitious revolution seeks only to change the form of government in the country in which it takes place. If it is also an anticolonial revolution, its external goal is simply to establish its country's independence within the existing international system. A highly ambitious revolution, by contrast, is one in which the internal goal becomes an external goal as well. Not satisfied with establishing its own form of revolutionary government at home, it actively encourages the establishment of similar revolutionary governments in other countries. Instead of accepting the existing system of international relations, an ambitious revolution seeks to transform it regionally or even globally.

REVOLUTIONARY WAVES

For the purposes of this study, revolutionary waves are groups of revolutions with similar objectives. How a revolution occurs is not important in determining which revolutionary wave a given revolution belongs to. This is because revolutions that take place by differing methods can accomplish similar goals. Marxist-Leninist regimes, for example, have been established not just by one method, but by several—rural revolution, urban revolution, coup d'état, and revolution from without.

By contrast, different revolutionary outcomes have been accomplished by similar revolutionary means. If we accept both McDaniel's argument about Russia and Farhi's argument about Nicaragua both being primarily urban revolutions, then urban revolution has resulted in the establishment of Marxist-Leninist and Islamic fundamentalist regimes, as well as democracies. Coups d'état have been used to establish a wide variety of regimes, including Marxist-Leninist, Arab nationalist, Islamic fundamentalist, and others.

A revolution can belong to more than one revolutionary wave. In addition to belonging to a particular "for" wave, it can also belong to one or more "against" waves. An "against" revolutionary wave consists of those revolutions that overthrew a particular form of government or socioeconomic system. "Against" revolutionary waves include antimonarchical, anticolonial, anticapitalist, anti-Western, and antidictatorial ones, among others.

Individual "against" revolutionary waves have not been associated with any one particular "for" wave. Antimonarchical revolutions have resulted in democratic as well as a wide variety of nondemocratic regimes, including narrowly nationalist, pannationalist (such as Arab nationalist), Marxist-Leninist, and Islamic fundamentalist coming to power. Similarly, the only commonality amongst postcolonial revolutionary states has been independence. Anticapitalist, antidemocratic, and anti-Western revolutions have also resulted in different types of "for" revolutions, including fascist, Marxist-Leninist, Arab nationalist, and Islamic fundamentalist. The wave of anti-Marxist-Leninist revolutions in 1989-91 has resulted in a variety of regimes, ranging from democratic to nondemocratic nationalist, procapitalist to anticapitalist, and pro-Western to anti-Western. In some cases, most notably in Russia, the exact nature of the post–Marxist-Leninist regime has not yet been decided and is being hotly contested by various internal forces. Even a revolutionary wave defined as broadly as "antidictatorial" does not imply a particular "for" revolution; some antidictatorial revolutions have resulted in democracy while others have resulted in yet another form of dictatorship.

A "for" revolutionary wave consists of those revolutions that established (or earnestly attempted to establish) a particular form of government or socioeconomic system, such as democracy, Marxism-Leninism, Arab nationalism, or Islamic fundamentalism. Just as there has been no uniformity in the kind of regime established in each "against" revolutionary wave, revolutions which have been "for" the same goal have been fought against a variety of opponents. The establishment of Marxist-Leninist regimes, for example, has not been associated with the overthrow of just one type of regime, but of several: monarchies, colonial rule, and other forms of dictatorship. Democratic revolutions have been fought against a variety of regimes as well.

Roles within a Revolutionary Wave

Just as there are different methods by which revolutions occur and different revolutionary objectives, there are also different roles within a revolutionary wave which revolutions play vis-à-vis one another.

A revolutionary wave can contain a *central revolution,* which articulates a vision of altering the existing international system by inspiring a series of revolutions similar to its own, and by acting as the center of this group of revolutionary states. In the Marxist-Leninist revolutionary wave, this role was played by the Soviet Union. In the Arab nationalist revolutionary wave, this role was played by Egypt. Iran has played this role in the Islamic fundamentalist revolutionary wave.

In these three instances, the central revolutionary states were also the first to experience their particular type of "for" revolution. This need not, however, always be the case. Italy was the first country to experience a fascist revolution, yet it was Nazi Germany that became the central revolutionary state within the fascist revolutionary wave.

In order to play the role of central revolution, a state must have the ability to be a great power on either a regional or global scale. Generally, the central revolution is the strongest state within a revolutionary wave.

But in order for there to be a revolutionary wave, there must also be other actual or potential revolutions. *Aspiring revolutionaries* are inspired by the central revolution, attempt to emulate it, and usually seek its assistance in coming to power. The existence of a central revolution and one or more aspiring revolutionary movements with serious prospects of success is the minimum requirement for there to be a nondemocratic "for" revolutionary wave that spreads primarily via affiliate revolutions. The success of central revolutions in Russia, Egypt, and Iran, as well as the rise of aspiring revolutionaries in many countries seeking to emulate them, was enough to convince the status quo powers that they were being confronted with a revolutionary wave even before any other such revolutions took place.

Not all aspiring revolutionaries, however, are successful. Those that are can have various relations with the central revolution. Revolutionary regimes set up by central revolutions in countries they have invaded are *subordinate* or puppet revolutions. By definition, of course, such subordinate revolutions do not voluntarily affiliate themselves with a central revolution. The existence of one or more revolutions subordinate to a central revolution, however, does not mean that other revolutions elsewhere cannot voluntarily affiliate themselves with a central revolution. Although most of the Marxist-Leninist regimes in Eastern Europe were installed by and subordinate to the Soviet Union, Marxist-Leninist regimes in the Third World voluntarily affiliated themselves with Moscow.

An *affiliate* revolution is one that comes to power by any method other than a revolution from without and in which the revolutionary government voluntarily aligns itself with the central revolution. Since the affiliation is voluntary, it can occur to different degrees, from tight to loose. A revolution need not occur completely without external involvement to qualify as an affiliate revolution: aspiring revolutionaries often have received military assistance from the central revolution, as well as other states in their revolutionary wave. Receiving military assistance from abroad does not make one revolution subordinate to another, as will be seen in chapter 3.

Affiliate revolutions can be either "ambitious" or "unambitious." An unambitious one is allied with the central revolution, but it does not actively spread the revolutionary wave itself. An ambitious affiliate revolution, by contrast, works actively to spread revolution to other countries while maintaining its alliance with the central revolution. Cuba played this role in the Marxist-Leninist revolutionary wave. Whether an affiliate revolution (or, for that matter, a central revolution) is ambitious or unambitious about expanding the revolutionary wave, however, is not necessarily a permanent status: a regime can be ambitious about spreading revolution at one point in time but become unambitious about it later, and vice versa.

Nor is being an affiliate revolution necessarily a permanent status. A revolution that voluntarily affiliates with a central revolution can also voluntarily *disaffiliate*. An affiliate may become disenchanted with a central revolution for a number of reasons, including the level of aid the affiliate receives from the central revolution, or its fear that the central revolution is trying to transform it into a subordinate revolution.

An unambitious disaffiliate revolution seeks to dissociate itself from the central revolution while retaining its own revolutionary regime. An ambitious disaffiliate revolution, however, not only dissociates itself but vies for leadership of the revolutionary wave. In other words, an ambitious disaffiliate revolution becomes a *rival* revolution. A dramatic example of this was China after the Sino-Soviet split. Beijing vied with Moscow for leadership of the Marxist-Leninist revolutionary wave as a whole. Not only did many Marxist revolutionary movements split into pro-Soviet and pro-Chinese wings, but Marxist regimes in Albania and Cambodia became affiliated with China.

Finally, there exist what can be called *unaffiliated* revolutions. This term can describe the relations between revolutions in the same "against" wave. Merely because two countries experienced antimonarchical or anticolonial revolutions, for example, does not mean that they are allied to each other or that they give more than rhetorical support, either together or separately, to furthering their common revolutionary wave. But a revolution can be part of the same "for" wave and yet be unaffiliated with the central revolution. There were, for example, a number of "socialist" revolutions in the Third World that partially adopted Marxist-Leninist rhetoric and practices but either did not affiliate or affiliated only tenuously with the Soviet Union. It is arguable, though, whether or not such revolutions should be considered part of the same revolutionary wave as the central revolution and its affiliates and/or subordinates. It is also important to distinguish between unaffiliated revolutions that were never linked to a central revolution and disaffiliated revolutions that once were but later severed that link.

Not all revolutionary waves contain all the revolutionary roles described here. Different waves exhibit different relationship patterns. In the antimonarchical and anticolonial revolutionary waves, there has been no central revolution with which states experiencing similar revolutions have affiliated. Indeed, the revolutions in these "against" waves are largely unaffiliated with one another. To the extent that they are affiliated, it is not by being part of the same "against" wave, but by being part of the same "for" wave.

In the democratic revolutionary wave, the United States can arguably be considered the central revolution. Whether it is or not, however, the predominant relationship among the members of this wave is that they are affiliated or unaffiliated with one another. Only in the unusual instance of a democratic revolution from without is there a subordinate revolution in this wave, and this subordinate status is, of necessity, temporary. For if a democratic revolution from without takes root, it voluntarily chooses whether to be affiliated or unaffiliated with other democracies. But if democratic revolution from without does not take root, then the country it is attempted in cannot be considered to be part of the democratic revolutionary wave.

The predominant pattern of relationships in nondemocratic "for" waves that expand via invasion is the existence of a central revolution and one or more subordinate revolutions. Such waves, though, can also include affiliate revolutions, as occurred in the fascist revolutionary wave (fascist Italy voluntarily affiliated with Nazi Germany). Nondemocratic revolutionary waves that expand primarily via affiliate revolutions, however, can contain a variety of roles including central, aspiring, affiliate, disaffiliate, rival, unaffiliated, and even subordinate revolutions.

LIFE SPANS OF REVOLUTIONARY WAVES

"Against" Waves

Revolutionary waves have exhibited different patterns of success over time. Certain waves, once begun, have spread and spread until they have engulfed virtually the entire world. One such "against" wave has been the wave of antimonarchical (or, more precisely, anti–absolute monarchical) revolutions. At the time of the American Revolution in 1776, virtually the entire world was ruled by absolute monarchs. At present, only a handful of absolute monarchies remain, almost all of which are in the Muslim world. Of course, not all absolute monarchies fell as a result of revolution. Some evolved slowly and relatively peacefully into constitutional monarchies or into some other form of democracy. Antimonarchical revolutions, though, do seem to have helped establish an international norm about absolute monarchy being illegitimate.

Another "against" wave that has enjoyed near-universal success has been that of anticolonial (or, more precisely, anti–European colonial) revolutions. The American Revolution was the first such revolution in the modern era that resulted in colonies establishing independence and being recognized by the status quo powers, including the ex-colonial ruler. At present, only a handful of European colonies remain, and these do so with the consent (often the insistence) of a majority of the people living in them, either because they see continued colonial rule to be economically beneficial or because they fear absorption by a neighboring state.

Not all colonies achieved independence as a result of revolution: many obtained it peacefully. As with antimonarchical revolutions, though, anticolonial revolutions seem to have been instrumental in establishing what has become a universally accepted norm: European colonial rule without the consent of the local majority is illegitimate.

Some other "against" revolutionary waves have proven more finite. A number of anticapitalist revolutions have sought to either isolate a given country from the international capitalist economy, or, more ambitiously, to create an alternative international economic system. For the most part, these anticapitalist projects came to an end either through the collapse of the revolutionary regimes pursuing them, or, more remarkably, through hitherto anticapitalist regimes' adopting capitalism and seeking to increase instead of decrease their participation in the international capitalist economy (China after 1976 is a dramatic example of this). Antidemocratic revolutions (revolutions overthrowing democratic governments) have proved short-lived in some countries and long-lived in others (most notably Franco's Spain). Samuel Huntington has observed that countries in which democracies have been overthrown have often successfully redemocratized later (Huntington 1991, 42-43, 270-71).[5] Antidemocratic revolution has not proven sustainable as a wave. Similarly, the anti-Western nature of many revolutions was often not sustained when, with the passage of time, revolutionary leaders or their successors found cooperation with the West to be desirable.

"For" Waves
The Democratic Revolutionary Wave
Unlike nondemocratic "for" revolutionary waves, which (I will argue) expand and then collapse, the democratic revolutionary wave is one that has spread and spread. The democratic "for" revolutionary wave, then, must be considered separately from its nondemocratic counterparts.

The English Revolution of the mid-seventeenth century could be considered the first attempted democratic revolution, though its results were ambiguous. The American Revolution of the late eighteenth century, by contrast, was an unambiguously democratic revolution. Since then, many other states have democratized through either revolutionary or evolutionary means. While there have been setbacks for democracy, especially in countries with little experience with it, by the late twentieth century the number of countries that have adopted and sustained democracy has become impressive. Like the antimonarchical and anticolonial revolutionary waves, the democratic one has also spread widely. Though democracy has been reversed in some countries in the past and there appear to be strong prospects for its being reversed in several countries (especially Russia and others in the former Soviet bloc) that have adopted it recently, the democratic revolutionary wave as a whole appears to be highly durable and is likely to remain so (Huntington 1991).

Some might question whether or not democratic transformations can be considered revolutionary. Democracy itself is a system that eschews revolutionary transformation. In several countries democracy has developed in a purely evolutionary manner (Canada, Australia, New

Zealand, and Norway). Yet democracy has been established by revolutionary means in many other countries, by rural revolution (the United States), urban revolution (East Germany, Poland, Czechoslovakia, Hungary, Bulgaria, Estonia, Latvia, and Lithuania), coup d'état (which, at least, initiated the democratic revolution in Portugal), revolution from above (Spain after Franco), and revolution from without (West Germany, Italy, and Japan after World War II). There have also been countries where democracy has developed fitfully via both revolution and evolution (Britain and France). Finally, there have been many instances in which dictatorships have suddenly lost legitimacy—even within the armed forces and bureaucracies running them—and a peaceful democratic transformation has taken place (Greece in 1974 and Argentina in 1982).

Like antimonarchical and anticolonial revolutions, democratic revolutions appear to have established a norm that became so widely held even in nondemocratic countries that after a certain point the concept had no serious opposition. Although Francis Fukuyama (1989) has predicted that this democratic norm is destined to spread to all countries, it must be noted that the democratic revolutionary wave has not yet gained the degree of near-universal success or acceptance that the antimonarchical and anticolonial revolutionary waves have. On the other hand, the democratic wave has differed markedly from nondemocratic "for" revolutionary waves in that none of the latter have included evolutionary cases.

While upholding democracy in their own countries, democratic governments have often been unenthusiastic about trying to export it to others. Indeed, the democratic governments of several countries have maintained nondemocratic colonial rule over many other nations in the not-too-distant past. But while Western public opinion as a whole saw no contradiction in this previously, this is no longer the case.

Despite their change of heart regarding direct colonial rule, some Western democratic governments—the United States in particular—have at times supported dictatorships or even acted to suppress democracy in other countries. And this has often (though not always) occurred with the acquiescence of the Western public. The protection of foreign policy interests (or perceived foreign policy interests) has often been more important to democratic governments than the spread of democracy. But the pursuit of foreign policy goals that contradict a state's ideological goals is not unique to democratic nations; governments of nondemocratic revolutionary waves have often displayed this behavior as well, as when the USSR supported Arab nationalist regimes that brutally suppressed Marxist-Leninist parties in their countries.

There have been occasions, though, when democratic governments have sought to export revolution by force. During the American Revolution, for example, a failed attempt was made to include Canada within the United States. Another attempt to incorporate Canada by force occurred during the War of 1812. The United States successfully used force to incorporate what was then northern Mexico in 1848. By contrast, the United States did not include within its democracy the territories it gained during the War of 1898, but ruled over the Philippines and Puerto Rico as colonies, and Cuba as a semicolony, instead.

In the mid-twentieth century, the established democracies began attempting to foster democratization in other countries. As was mentioned before, successful revolutions from without brought democracy to West Germany, Italy, and Japan at the end of World War II. The British and the French attempted to erect some form of democracy in most, though not all, of the colonies to which they granted independence in the mid twentieth century.

Especially since the mid-1980s, the United States has assisted to a greater or lesser extent the democratic transformations that occurred in a number of countries where Washington had previously supported dictatorships: the Philippines (1986), South Korea (1987-88), Chile (1988), El Salvador (1992), and Haiti (1986 and 1994) (Smith 1994, 266-307). The United States, however, is not the only Western government that has facilitated transitions from dictatorship to democracy; several West European governments, as well as the (then) European Community, played key roles in assisting such transitions in Southern Europe in the 1970s and in Eastern Europe in the late 1980s (Pridham 1991; Pridham 1994).

Democracy, though, is not a system of government that can be exported from one country to another without the importer's consent and cooperation. Even though West Germany, Italy, and Japan were occupied by Western forces at the end of World War II, democracy could not have taken root without the participation of the citizenry in these countries. The conviction that democracy needs strong internal roots to survive may in part explain why the European powers did not intervene to restore democracy in their former colonies where democracy had been overthrown after independence.

During the 1980s, the U.S. government created something akin to a "Democrintern" through the establishment of a bureaucracy dedicated to the promotion of democratization abroad. This "democracy bureaucracy" (the National Endowment for Democracy, new offices created within the

U.S. Agency for International Development, and the organizations through which they channel their assistance) acts primarily in support of organizations seeking progress toward democratization—including hitherto authoritarian governments. The U.S. government has also played an important role in assisting transitions to democracy through arranging for the less-than-voluntary departure of a dictator. At times, the United States has intervened militarily to oust a dictatorship and has organized a democratic revolution from without (Grenada, 1983; Panama, 1989; and Haiti, 1994). The United States, however, has not supported democratization equally everywhere. Far from encouraging democratization, the United States has sought to protect dictatorial regimes in certain countries, such as Saudi Arabia and Oman, which have been deemed to be especially important for U.S. security interests. America's degree of ambitiousness about exporting revolution, then, has been inconsistent and ambiguous.

The extent to which U.S. government actions have been of crucial or only marginal importance to the success of democratization in other countries is hotly debated among scholars.[6] This debate, however, will not be discussed here as it does not fall within the scope of my study.

Nondemocratic "For" Revolutionary Waves
Nondemocratic "for" revolutionary waves, by contrast, have sometimes been highly ambitious in terms of their desire—indeed, their determination—to spread a particular type of revolution elsewhere. Many nondemocratic revolutions, however, have not had this ambition.

The Turkish Revolution led by Kemal Ataturk completely renounced the empire that the Ottoman regime had sought to maintain. Although "nationalist" revolution may be considered a type of "for" wave, nations usually experience their own type of nationalism not linked to—in fact, usually opposed to—other nations. Revolutionary nationalism (such as that of Turkey, Mexico, or Burma) can come in the form of a country whose revolutionary regime has no ambition to export its type of revolution, but is concerned instead with removing and keeping out what it considers to be hostile foreign influence. Such revolutions can be described as a revolutionary wave consisting solely of a central revolution. Nationalist revolutions can also have the limited ambition of exporting their revolution to parts of one or more neighboring countries that they claim rightfully belong to the "homeland." But as threatening as such claims may be to neighboring countries, these limited nationalist ambitions must be distinguished from the highly ambitious revolutionary waves that seek to spread throughout an entire region or even the world.

There have been two types of highly ambitious nondemocratic "for" revolutionary waves: 1) those that expand primarily via invasion; and 2) those that expand primarily via affiliate revolution. Some revolutionary waves, of course, have employed both methods of expansion. Usually, though, one or the other method of expansion has been predominant, or one method has been predominant at one time in a particular geographic area while the other has been predominant later elsewhere.

These two types have had finite life spans. Both experience expansion followed by contraction. Each, however, experiences a distinct pattern of expansion and contraction.

Nondemocratic Revolutionary Waves That Expand via Invasion

While extremely dramatic, the life span and pattern of expansion and contraction of a nondemocratic revolutionary wave that expands primarily through invasion is relatively simple. The central revolutionary regime invades other countries and either incorporates them directly within its own territory or sets up subordinate revolutionary regimes in them. This type of revolutionary wave is halted through the balance of power. Often fearing that not just their vital interests but their very existence is at stake, the status quo powers eventually band together in an alliance. At minimum, the alliance serves to prevent further expansion by invasion. More ambitiously, the alliance wages war against the revolutionary wave to roll it back from one or more countries where it expanded and then acts to prevent reexpansion from the central revolution. At maximum, the alliance not only rolls back the expansion, but also destroys the wave altogether by bringing an end to the central revolutionary regime.

The French Revolution was at the center of the first highly ambitious revolutionary wave that expanded primarily by invasion. It is important to distinguish between the ideals of "liberty, equality, fraternity" expressed by the French revolutionaries and by later revolutionaries in France and elsewhere, and the actual nature of the various French revolutionary regimes between 1789 and 1815. Whether it was under the Jacobins, the Directory, or Napoleon, the French revolutionary regimes espoused democracy but were in fact highly authoritarian. Under Napoleon, France exported its revolution via invasion: it invaded other countries and replaced many of their governments with ones which were nominally independent but in fact subordinate to Paris. After years of fighting, the status quo powers halted the French advance, drove French forces out of the countries

Napoleon had conquered, and restored the Bourbon monarchy to power in France (Brinton 1965, 192; Holtman 1967, 64-71).

The fascist revolutionary wave also expanded primarily by invasion, though it contained some affiliate revolutions too. The fascist wave began with the rise of Mussolini in 1922. Independent fascist revolutions subsequently took place in a number of other countries, including Portugal, Japan, Germany, and Spain (this last one took place with military assistance from Italy and Germany). Hitler also managed to persuade even the status quo powers that his revolutionary efforts were limited to the incorporation of predominantly German-speaking areas into Germany—until 1939, when his forces invaded Czechoslovakia beyond the Sudetenland and then Poland. It was at this point that Hitler, in alliance with Mussolini, launched his effort to spread fascism to the rest of Europe by force. Japan's goals also expanded from conquering Manchuria (which it occupied in 1931) to invading the rest of China in 1937, and Southeast Asia and many of the Pacific islands in 1941. By 1945, the Allied powers had defeated and occupied the three major fascist countries. None of the subordinate fascist regimes survived. Nonexpansionary affiliate fascist regimes, however, did survive for thirty years more in Portugal (which disaffiliated itself from German and Italian ambitions during World War II) and Spain (which, although it sent troops to fight against the Soviet Union, disaffiliated itself with the German and Italian war effort against the Western powers).

The Marxist-Leninist revolutionary wave expanded both by invasion and by affiliate revolution. An initial wave of expansion by invasion occurred when Bolshevik forces recaptured most (but not all) of the non-Russian areas of the former tsarist empire that had asserted their independence in the years just after the 1917 revolution. Moscow also employed invasion to export Marxist-Leninist revolution to Mongolia in 1920. After World War II, the USSR oversaw Marxist-Leninist revolutions from without in virtually all the areas of Eastern Europe that its forces had occupied. It was export of revolution by invasion that led to the formation of the North Atlantic Treaty Organization (NATO) to contain the further expansion of the Marxist-Leninist revolutionary wave in Europe.

The Soviet Union also occupied North Korea at the end of World War II and oversaw a Marxist-Leninist revolution from without there. It was the North Korean effort to expand the Marxist-Leninist revolutionary wave to South Korea by invasion in 1950 that resulted in the American-led military effort that repulsed it. While the United States failed to achieve the more ambitious goal of destroying North Korea's Marxist-Leninist regime, it succeeded in both preserving the non-Marxist regime in the South and solidifying security relationships with a number of other countries in the region that feared the USSR.

The creation of American-led military alliances in Europe and the Far East served to contain the further expansion of the Marxist-Leninist revolutionary wave by invasion in these two regions. These containment efforts, though, did not halt the expansion of this revolutionary wave through affiliate revolution to many Third World countries.

On a smaller scale, the Iraqi attack on Iran in 1980 and occupation of Kuwait in 1990 were attempts by Saddam Hussein to spread the Iraqi Ba'thist version of Arab nationalist revolution via invasion. Iran was able to thwart this effort primarily with its own resources, though it did receive some support from the status quo powers that did not want Iraq to succeed. Kuwait, on the other hand, was too small and weak to avoid being completely overrun by Iraqi forces in a very short period of time. Because the status quo powers did not want Saddam Hussein to retain control of Kuwait's vast oil reserves—or to acquire control over even more of the region's oil through further spread of its revolution—an American-led alliance was created under UN auspices to protect Saudi Arabia and push Iraqi forces back out of Kuwait. While the revolutionary regime led by Saddam Hussein remained in power in Iraq after being expelled from Kuwait, its ability to export revolution by invasion was greatly diminished as a result.

Nondemocratic Revolutionary Waves That Expand via Affiliate Revolution

Compared to the life span of nondemocratic "for" revolutionary waves that expand primarily via invasion, the life span of nondemocratic "for" revolutionary waves that expand primarily via affiliate revolution is far more complex. Having discussed revolutions and revolutionary waves in general in this chapter, I will devote the rest of the book to examining the more complicated life span, as well as pattern of expansion and contraction, of this second type of nondemocratic revolutionary wave.

In order to avoid constant repetition of their outsize labels, I will refer to the two types of nondemocratic "for" revolutionary waves from this point onward as simply nondemocratic revolutionary waves that expand via invasion and ones that expand via affiliate revolution.

Chapter 2

The Central Revolution and Aspiring Revolutions

The revolutionary regimes that came to power in Russia in 1917, Egypt in 1952, and Iran in 1979 all had an extraordinary expectation. They thought that their revolutions were so attractive that movements would rise up in other nations seeking to carry out similar revolutions. What was even more extraordinary, however, is the extent to which this expectation was fulfilled: revolutionary movements did indeed arise that sought to deliberately emulate the revolutionary example of Russia, Egypt, or Iran.

The Marxist-Leninist revolutionary wave was played out on a global scale. In addition to the central revolution in Russia itself and the subordinate revolutions that Soviet armed forces brought to neighboring countries (Mongolia in 1920 and Eastern Europe and North Korea at the end of World War II), affiliate Marxist-Leninist revolutions came to power in Yugoslavia and Albania (1944), China (1949), North Vietnam (1954), Cuba (1959), the Congo (1964, 1968), South Yemen (1967), Benin (1972), Ethiopia and Guinea-Bissau (1974), Cambodia, South Vietnam, Laos, Madagascar, Cape Verde, Mozambique, and Angola (1975), Afghanistan (1978), and Grenada and Nicaragua (1979). In addition, strong Marxist-Leninist revolutionary movements rose up in a number of other Third World countries where they fought for many years, but did not succeed in coming to power.

The Arab nationalist revolutionary wave was limited in terms of its ambitions to the Middle East, but it swept dramatically through this region in the 1950s and 1960s. After the central revolution in Egypt, affiliate revolutions took place in Syria and Iraq (1958), Algeria and North Yemen (1962), and Sudan and Libya (1969). Yasir Arafat, a leader in the Arab nationalist mold, has dominated the Palestinian movement from the mid-1960s until the present. Other Arab nationalist movements attempted to seize power elsewhere in the Arab world—including Saudi Arabia—but did not succeed.

The Islamic revolutionary wave is occurring not only in the Middle East, but also in Central Asia and elsewhere in the Muslim world. It began with the Iranian Revolution. Since then, additional Islamic fundamentalist revolutions have occurred in Sudan (1989) and Afghanistan (1992, 1996). There are also significant Islamic revolutionary movements in Egypt, Algeria, Tunisia, the West Bank and Gaza, Lebanon, Syria, Iraq, Saudi Arabia, Bahrain, Oman, Tajikistan, and other Muslim countries.

This chapter focuses on the relationship between the central revolution and aspiring revolutions within these three revolutionary waves. It will examine the common features of the three central revolutions and the ideologies they espoused, the role established revolutionary regimes have played in assisting aspiring revolutionaries come to power, the appeal of internationalist revolutionary ideologies to revolutionaries in other countries, the differences that can arise between central revolutions and aspiring revolutions up to the point they come to power, and the prospects that the Islamic fundamentalist revolutionary wave will expand further.

CENTRAL REVOLUTIONS AND REVOLUTIONARY IDEOLOGIES

Despite the many significant differences in their ideologies and historical development, the revolutions that occurred in Russia, Egypt, and Iran had some elements in common. All three were antimonarchical. All three were also anti-Western. All three took place in countries that had once been great powers, but that at the time of their revolutions had become weakened vis-à-vis the West (Russia) or had become its clients (Egypt and Iran). In all three cases, the revolutionary leaderships that came to power articulated their own ideologies which, they were confident, would spark similar revolutions in other countries.[1]

What were the expectations of these revolutionaries? The leader of the Russian Revolution, V.I. Lenin, expected Marxism-Leninism to spread to the entire world. He saw the primary division in the world being economic class: the haves versus the have-nots. The have-nots, led by the proletariat, would triumph over the haves, led by the bourgeoisie. While Lenin believed the competitive rigors of capitalism would ultimately lead to the breakdown of solidarity among the bourgeoisie of different countries, he also believed that international class solidarity would command the loyalty of the proletariat of all countries to a far greater extent than nationalism. He also believed that class peace in the most industrialized states of the West (where Marx had predicted socialist revolution would occur) had been bought through imperialism. It was the exploitation of colonies and semicolonies by the bourgeoisie of the industrialized states that allowed them to maintain an artificially high standard of living for their workers and thus avoid socialist revolution, according to Lenin's understanding of economics. But if the West could be deprived of its colonies and semicolonies through anticolonial revolutions, Lenin expected that socialist revolution in the West would follow (Kolakowski 1978, 491-93; MacFarlane 1985, 28-30).

Initially, Lenin believed that socialist revolution in Russia alone would be enough to immediately spark socialist revolution in the West. When it became clear that this expectation would not be fulfilled, Lenin organized the Comintern—the Communist International (1919-43)—to guide the revolutionary efforts of other Communist parties. While also encouraging communist activity in the West, Lenin continued to stress revolution in what later became known as the Third World—the "weakest link in the chain of capitalism." Lenin believed it was not even necessary for revolution in the Third World to be socialist to undermine the West; even "bourgeois nationalist" revolution there would suffice to undermine Western economies, though he expected that the Third World nations where bourgeois nationalist revolution took place would ultimately experience Marxist-Leninist revolution also (Rubinstein 1988, 15-16).

Except for Stalin during the Depression of the 1930s, it is unclear whether subsequent Soviet leaders thought Marxist-Leninist revolution in the West was actually likely. But again, except for Stalin after his failed effort to promote Marxist-Leninist revolution in China during the 1920s, Soviet leaders before Gorbachev saw Third World countries as being ripe for revolution and thought that such revolutions would serve to weaken the Western powers even if they did not bring about their demise (Katz 1982; MacFarlane 1990).

The foremost Arab nationalist leader, Jamal 'Abd al-Nasir, drew his inspiration from the Arab caliphates that arose in the period after the Prophet Muhammad, and under which the entire Arab world and beyond was united in a single Arab-led government. The Arab nationalist vision called for ridding the Arab world of all foreign influences, including monarchies and other pro-Western regimes as well as the new state of Israel, which was regarded as the artificial creation of British imperialism. Further, the Arab nationalist vision called for the elimination of all borders between Arab states which they saw as having been arbitrarily drawn by the British and the French to demarcate their spheres of influence. The continued existence of these borders, it was argued, served only the Western imperialist goal of keeping the Arabs divided and weak. Arab unity, by contrast, would lead to Arab strength vis-à-vis the rest of the world. The Arab nationalist economic program borrowed heavily from Marxism-Leninism and looked upon the USSR as an ally, but nonalignment between the superpowers was to be the basis of Arab nationalist foreign policy (Nasser 1955).

The Iranian revolutionary leader, Ayatollah Ruhollah Khomeini, envisioned the spread of Islamic revolution beyond Iran to other countries. What he regarded as the natural limits to the spread of Islamic revolution, though, were not clear. At minimum, he saw Islamic revolution spreading to predominantly Muslim countries. But he also envisioned the Islamic revolution appealing to the "oppressed" everywhere, though he did not spell out what the relationship between the Islamic revolution and the non-Islamic oppressed was to be. On occasion, he seemed to envision the spread of Islam beyond the countries that currently have a predominantly Muslim population to others through conversion—much like the initial spread of Islam from the Arabian Peninsula outward. In practice, though, his aspirations for further Islamic revolution focused on the countries in the immediate vicinity of Iran. He particularly wanted to see Muslim governments allied either with the United States or the USSR ousted and replaced by Islamic regimes. Khomeini regarded the government of Saudi Arabia as being especially iniquitous not only for being an absolute monarchy (a form of rule he regarded as alien to Islam), but also for posing as a just Islamic government dutifully protecting the Muslim holy cities of Mecca and Medina while actually, in his view, serving the interests of "the Great Satan"—the United States (Bakhash 1984, 233-34; Piscatori 1986, 111-13).

These three ideologies served several functions for the revolutionaries espousing them. They provided an analytical framework for identifying the ills of their societies, a justification for revolution, and a general program of action once it occurred. This function, of course, could have been served through the adoption of some other revolutionary ideology that had been successful in other states. The revolutionaries who formulated these ideologies, however, intended to launch not just a revolution, but a revolutionary wave in which their nation would play the central role. The Russian and Iranian revolutionaries each envisioned their nation as being the leader of an alliance of similar revolutionary states. The Egyptian revolutionaries were in a sense more ambitious still: instead of seeking to be the leader of a revolutionary alliance, they sought the unification of the Arab world into one huge state to be ruled from Cairo. In all three cases, then, the leaders of central revolutions sought not just internal political change, but also the transformation of their nations from relatively weak states into great powers.

Further, these ideologies allowed the central revolutionary states to play the role of a great power very quickly. After their revolutions, Russia, Egypt, and Iran were not militarily stronger than they were before. Indeed, Russia and Iran were arguably weaker in military terms. What made others fear or hope (depending on their point of view) that these nations had become great powers after their revolutions was the possibility that their ideologies appealed to others. Even without great military strength, the central revolutions used the appeal of these ideologies as a powerful weapon to strike out against the interests of the status quo powers. And to the extent that their ideologies resonated abroad, the international importance of the central revolutionary states was indeed magnified.

The leaderships of the central revolutions believed that it was the "internationalist" aspect of their ideologies that would allow them to gain adherents in other countries. The Russian revolutionaries expected their Marxist-Leninist ideology to appeal to the "workers of all countries." The Iranian revolutionaries sought to appeal to "true Muslims" everywhere. Even Arab nationalism was internationalist in the sense that it sought to transcend the individual Arab states (Egypt, Syria, Iraq, etc.) and appeal to all Arabs.

In addition, the internationalist aspect of these three ideologies played an important role in gaining adherents to the revolutionary wave not only abroad, but also domestically. Before the 1917 revolution, the Russian tsars expanded the territory under their control by absorbing many non-Russian nations into their empire. As with colonized nations elsewhere, nationalist sentiment rose up among these non-Russian nations. In contrast to many other Russian groups that opposed tsarist rule but insisted on keeping the empire intact, Lenin decried the plight of the non-Russians in the Russian empire and called for non-Russians to be granted their independence if that is what they chose (Nahaylo and Swoboda 1990, 14-19).

But Lenin, in fact, did not want to see the breakup of the Russian empire. Although many non-Russian nations declared their independence shortly after the Bolshevik coup, Lenin and his colleagues set about reabsorbing as much of the old tsarist empire as they could after temporarily ceding an enormous amount of territory in early 1918 under German pressure before the Kaiser's regime collapsed later that same year.

The Bolsheviks justified the reimposition of Russian rule over the non-Russians in terms of Marxist-Leninist ideology. For while Lenin was theoretically willing to allow non-Russian nations the right to secede, he claimed to believe that proletarian non-Russians would not want to do so. Those non-Russian nations that did declare their independence, then, must necessarily be under "bourgeois" control from which it was the duty of the proletariat in Russia to rescue them through military intervention. This argument seems highly cynical in retrospect, but at the time it was fervently accepted by many non-Russian Marxist-Leninists who actively cooperated in the imposition of Bolshevik rule from Moscow in their non-Russian republics. Stalin would later reward the loyalty of many of these non-Russian Marxist-Leninists with death or imprisonment (Nahaylo and Swoboda 1990, 18-80).

The rulers of Persia had also acquired control over many nations, though by the early twentieth century much of the territory Iran once possessed in the Caucasus and Central Asia had been lost to the Russian empire. But even within its shrunken twentieth-century borders, Iran contained a number of ethnic groups that had a territorial base on the borderlands of the country: Azeris in the northwest, Kurds in the west, Arabs in the southwest, Turkmen in the northeast, and Baluchis in the southeast (McLachlan 1994, 1). Like the Marxist-Leninist revolutionaries who inherited the tsarist empire, the Islamic fundamentalist revolutionaries who inherited the Persian empire sought to prevent secession on the part of minority national groups. As David Armstrong observed, Khomeini's "emphasis on the unity of all Muslims and the irrelevance of nationality held a clear message for separatist movements in Iran itself" (1993, 194).

Unlike the Russian and Persian empires, Egypt did not possess regionally dominant minority ethnic groups. As Adeed Dawisha put it, "Egypt, even under Ottoman and British control, had always constituted, and had always been perceived as, a single identifiable social and political unit" (1986, 42). Egypt, though, did contain one sizeable minority group: the Coptic Christians, variously estimated at between 10 and 20 percent of the Egyptian population. The Copts, however, were a minority everywhere in Egypt; there was no part of the country where they formed a majority. Nevertheless, the ideology of Arab nationalism did play an important role domestically in Egypt (and even more so in certain other Arab countries) through its uniting Muslims and Christians in their Arabness.

The ideologies of the central revolutions, then, furnished the justification for revolution, served to boost the international status of the countries they emerged in by making them the head of a revolutionary wave, and (more in Russia and Iran than in Egypt) provided a rationale for the continued cohesion of a diverse population inside one state.

Central Revolutions and the Expansion of Revolutionary Waves

To what extent have central revolutionary states been instrumental in assisting aspiring revolutionaries affiliated with them come to power? For aspiring revolutionaries, the most relevant form of external aid to examine is military assistance since nonmilitary assistance (economic, educational, political) to them either does not exist, cannot be measured satisfactorily, or is only marginally relevant. Economic assistance is something that goes to established governments; revolutionary movements with at best tenuous control over territory are not in a position to make use of it. The CIA used to publish figures on the numbers of students from different Third World countries pursuing higher education in the USSR, but there was no indication of how many of these became Marxist-Leninist revolutionaries.[2] Political assistance is a highly nebulous concept; it was often seen by aspiring revolutionaries as a euphemism for a central revolutionary regime's not giving them sufficient military assistance. Military assistance alone, then, will be considered here since it is the one form of assistance that aspiring revolutionaries can actually put to use in their quest for power.

But military assistance to aspiring revolutionaries cannot be measured precisely since reliable data is not available. Although Soviet archives have become increasingly open, they are not completely so. Hard information on sensitive subjects, such as arms transfers to revolutionaries, remains elusive. The archives for Arab nationalist and Islamic fundamentalist regimes are even less accessible, and so precise information about the extent to which states in these revolutionary waves have aided their fellow revolutionaries elsewhere is even more difficult to obtain. Western estimates exist, of course, but these are also not completely reliable. This is partly because the U.S. intelligence services, from which these estimates usually originate, do not wish to release detailed information that might compromise their sources, and partly because these sources (especially in the past, before high resolution satellite photography was available) usually could not provide precise information.

Yet despite the imprecise nature of the data, general information is available about the extent to which revolutionary regimes within all three waves gave military assistance to aspiring revolutionaries. Though the figures may not be precisely accurate, enough is known in general terms to state whether aspiring revolutionaries received major, significant, minor, or no military assistance from established revolutionary regimes. It is these terms (major, significant, minor, or no military assistance) that will be used here since, ironically, their imprecision is a more accurate reflection of what is known than the false precision of dollar or other numerical estimates. The assistance aspiring revolutionaries received before they came to power will be discussed here; what assistance affiliate revolutions received after coming to power will be examined in the next chapter.

In the Marxist-Leninist revolutionary wave, aspiring revolutionaries in countries where affiliate Marxist-Leninist revolutions eventually succeeded received varying degrees of assistance from the USSR and other Marxist-Leninist regimes. The first four affiliate revolutions took place in countries that had been occupied by Axis powers during World War II: Yugoslavia, Albania, China, and North Vietnam.

The Yugoslav Revolution received major assistance from the USSR: Soviet troops joined with Josip Broz Tito's Partisans in capturing Belgrade from the departing Germans in October 1944. In no other affiliate revolution did Soviet ground forces engage in combat. Nevertheless, the Yugoslav Revolution cannot be said to be a revolution from without like others in Eastern Europe: by the time the Germans were expelled, Tito's Partisans numbered 800,000 men. Further, after helping them capture Belgrade, Soviet forces moved out of northern Yugoslavia into Central Europe, leaving Tito in control of the country (Jelavich 1983, 271, 295).

The Albanian Marxist-Leninists appear to have received no help from the USSR, though they received major assistance from the Yugoslav Communists in establishing their organization and outmaneuvering rival anticommunist opposition forces (Jelavich 1983, 275-76, 297-98).

Soviet assistance to the Chinese Marxist-Leninists in 1949 was minor at best. While the Chinese Marxist-Leninists received some captured Japanese weaponry from the Soviets, the Soviets held back major weapons systems, destroying some and removing others to the USSR. What is more,

Stalin advised Mao to stop the war and compromise with the nationalist Kuomintang government during 1945-47. In 1948, when Mao's forces were gaining ground, Stalin advised him to halt his advance at the Yangtze river and settle for ruling part of China. Mao, however, did not heed Stalin's advice; his forces captured all of China except Taiwan in 1949 (MacFarlane 1990, 24-25).

Moscow did nothing to block the return of the French to Indochina after World War II. Indeed, the Democratic Republic of Vietnam declared by Ho Chi Minh in 1945 was not even recognized by Moscow until January 1950, and only then after Mao's new government in China had recognized it first. Despite its seeming public indifference, however, the USSR did provide minor assistance via China to help the Vietnamese Communists fight the French until their departure in 1954. Even then, Moscow pressed Ho to accept rule over North Vietnam while a non-Marxist regime was set up in the South (Pike 1987, 31-33, 41-42).

Fidel Castro was the first leader of a Marxist-Leninist revolution who had not risen up through the Comintern ranks. He appears to have received no support from the USSR or any other Marxist-Leninist group (including the Cuban Communist party) in his rise to power in 1959 (MacFarlane 1990, 29-30).

In South Yemen, Moscow encouraged cooperation between the rival Arab nationalist and Marxist-Leninist revolutionary groups. The two groups united in early 1966 but split and began fighting each other by the end of the year. Forced to choose between them, Moscow favored the Arab nationalist Front for the Liberation of South Yemen (FLOSY) that Egypt (which Moscow was courting) supported over the Marxist-Leninist National Liberation Front (NLF). With the large Egyptian military presence in neighboring North Yemen (where it was helping that country's Arab nationalist revolutionary regime fight off the as-yet undefeated royalist opposition), the bulk of Soviet weapons that flowed from North to South went to FLOSY. FLOSY, though, was doubly weakened in 1967—in North Yemen, when 'Abd al-Nasir withdrew his forces, and in South Yemen, when the British focused their military efforts more on FLOSY than on the NLF. With the final departure of the British from South Yemen in November 1967, the Marxist-Leninist NLF came to power despite Soviet actions, not because of them (Katz 1986, 74-75).

Moscow apparently had no role in the Marxist-Leninist coups that took place in the Congo (1964 and 1968) and Benin (1972). In Ethiopia, the USSR and its allies had provided some military assistance to Marxist guerrillas seeking independence for the coastal region, Eritrea, but not to the Marxist Ethiopian army officers who overthrew Emperor Haile Selassie in 1974 (Limberg 1990, 85-86; Patman 1990, 172-73).

The USSR and China competed in providing military assistance to North Vietnam's effort, which succeeded in 1975, to spread Marxist-Leninist revolution to the rest of Indochina. But whereas Moscow and Beijing provided roughly equal levels of assistance to Hanoi in the 1950s, by the mid-1970s the USSR and its East European allies were providing North Vietnam with 85 percent of its external military assistance while China was only providing 15 percent (Pike 1987, 106, 139, 196). Although there were indigenous Marxist-Leninist elements in South Vietnam and Laos, these revolutions owed their success primarily to the North Vietnamese armed forces (as well as to Soviet and Chinese arms) and should be considered revolutions from without. South Vietnam was absorbed into North Vietnam, and the regime that came to power in Laos was heavily dependent on Hanoi. North Vietnamese forces played an instrumental role in creating the conditions for the ouster of the pro-American Lon Nol regime in Cambodia by the Marxist-Leninist Khmer Rouge, but this group was definitely not subordinate to Hanoi.

The USSR and Cuba provided minor military assistance to Marxist-Leninist revolutionary groups fighting against Portuguese colonial rule in Angola, Guinea-Bissau, Cape Verde, and Mozambique from the 1960s until 1974. Following the 1974 coup d'etat, which toppled the right-wing regime in Lisbon, Portugal's decision to withdraw from its colonies provided an important boost to the Marxist-Leninists in these countries. In Guinea-Bissau, Mozambique, and Cape Verde, the Marxist-Leninist revolutionary groups did not face any serious rivals and thus were able to come to power easily. In Angola, however, the pro-Soviet Popular Movement for the Liberation of Angola (MPLA) did face a challenge from two other groups—the National Front for the Liberation of Angola (FNLA) and the National Union for the Total Independence of Angola (UNITA). Major support from Cuba and significant support from the USSR allowed the MPLA to fight off American- and South African-backed challenges from its rivals in 1975-76 (Golan 1988, 269-71).

Direct Soviet involvement in the April 1978 coup d'etat that brought a Marxist-Leninist regime to power in Afghanistan was relatively minor at most (Bradsher 1985, 82-84). Similarly, Cuba may have played a minor role (and the Soviets no role) in the March 1979 Marxist-Leninist coup in Grenada (Valenta and Valenta 1986, 5). The Sandinista rebels in Nicaragua received significant military assistance from Cuba in the final months of the successful revolution that brought them to power in Nicaragua during the summer of 1979 (Rubinstein 1988, 176; Limberg 1990, 98-99).

There were seven successful revolutions within the Arab national-ist revolutionary wave: Egypt (1952), Syria (1958), Iraq (1958), Alge-ria (1962), North Yemen (1962), Sudan (1969), and Libya (1969). In five of these cases (Egypt, Syria, Iraq, Sudan, and Libya), there was no oppor-tunity for external assistance to the aspiring revolutionaries since they came to power via coups d'etat. The 1962 Arab nationalist revolution in North Yemen also occurred via coup d'etat, but Egypt was significantly involved by providing the aspiring Yemeni revolutionaries with assurances of mili-tary aid in advance of the coup, a factor that may have been instrumental in their decision to launch it. Indeed, thousands of Egyptian troops began to arrive in Yemen only a week after the September 1962 coup (Stookey 1978, 231). As I have mentioned, Egypt backed an aspiring Arab na-tionalist revolutionary group against British rule in neighboring South Yemen, but it was defeated by a rival Marxist-Leninist revolutionary group in 1967.

Algeria was the only country in which Arab nationalist revolutionar-ies did not come to power through a coup d'etat, but via a guerrilla war that lasted from 1954 to 1962. Despite Egyptian claims that it was provid-ing major military assistance to the National Liberation Front (FLN)—claims that the French government accepted at face value—the aid Cairo actually supplied can only be described as minor (Horne 1977, 85, 129, 158, 164). The FLN received far more significant assistance from neighboring Tunisia after the latter achieved independence in 1956 (Horne 1977, 248).

Algeria would later provide significant military assistance to the POLISARIO Front, the Arab nationalist revolutionary group that has un-successfully sought independence for Western Sahara—the former Span-ish colony that was reabsorbed into Morocco (a pro-Western Arab monarchy) after Madrid withdrew in 1975. Finally, despite varying de-grees of assistance from Arab nationalist regimes and other countries, the predominantly Arab nationalist Palestine Liberation Organization (PLO) was unable to force Israel to withdraw from any of the Arab territories it came to occupy during the June 1967 Arab-Israeli War, much less the more ambitious goal of destroying the Jewish state altogether.

In the first few years following the Iranian Revolution, the Shi'ite clergy who had come to power in Tehran attempted to spread the Islamic revolutionary wave through supporting Shi'ite opposition movements in places where there were large Arab Shi'ite populations: Iraq, Kuwait, the al-Hasa province of Saudi Arabia, Bahrain, and Lebanon. The strongest effort was made in Iraq. Iraq had invaded Iran in September 1980 with the intention of, at minimum, seizing Iran's predominantly Arab province of Khuzistan. After Iranian forces pushed the Iraqis out of most of the territory they had seized, Iranian forces crossed over into Iraq. The Iranian government called for the downfall of Saddam Hussein and set up in Tehran an embryo Iraqi Islamic fundamentalist regime—the Supreme Council of the Islamic Revolution of Iraq (Bakhash 1984, 232-33). This effort, however, came to an end when Ayatollah Khomeini finally agreed to a cease-fire with Iraq in 1988.

Elsewhere, the 1979-80 Shi'ite riots in al-Hasa (Saudi Arabia) were easily quashed (Munson 1988, 72-74), as was a coup attempt in Bahrain in 1981 by a Shi'ite group that had reportedly received training in Iran (Bakhash 1984, 235).[3] In Lebanon, the Iranian government did play an instrumental role in supporting the buildup of a powerful Shi'ite revolutionary movement—the Hizballah—but while this group has become an important player in Lebanon's factional politics, it has not been strong enough to actually take power (Ajami 1992, 239-41).

Although Iran has been unsuccessful in promoting Islamic revolution by Arab Shi'ites, Islamic revolutions have succeeded in two predominantly Sunni countries: Sudan and Afghanistan. Iran appears to have had no role at all in the 1989 coup d'etat that brought an Islamic regime to power in Sudan. Sudan has its own tradition of Islamic revolt dating back to the 1880s Mahdist movement, which drove the British out of the country until 1898. Sadiq al-Mahdi—a great-grandson of the nineteenth century Mahdi—came to head a political party and serve as prime minister in the 1960s and 1980s. His Islamic democratic government was ousted in the 1989 Islamic fundamentalist coup by the army in cooperation with Dr. Hasan Turabi's National Islamic Front, which had begun as a branch of the Egyptian-based Muslim Brotherhood movement in the 1940s (Ayubi 1991, 104-13; Voll 1991, 374, 390, 394).

Iran did provide modest military assistance to the Afghan mujahadin fighting Soviet forces and the Marxist-Leninist regime in that country. Tehran, however, mainly supported groups representing the minority Shi'ite population in Afghanistan, which were not as powerful as the Sunni opposition forces (Fuller 1991, 228-30). Far more than anything Iran provided, it was the major military assistance from the United States and its allies which allowed these Sunni opposition forces to establish an Islamic revolutionary regime in Afghanistan in 1992. Nor did Iran support the Sunni Islamic fundamentalist (and highly anti-Shi'ite) Taliban, which took over most of Afghanistan (including the capital) in 1996. Indeed, the Iranian press accused the Taliban of being allied to the United States.[4]

There is a debate among Western observers over the extent to which Iran has continued to support Islamic fundamentalist revolution in other countries since the death of Ayatollah Khomeini. Since 1989, President Rafsanjani's government had greatly reduced Iranian support to Islamic revolutionaries in other countries, according to Said Amir Arjomand (1991, 63-66), John Esposito (1992, 151), and Ervand Abrahamian (1993, 141). According to Mark Juergensmeyer, however, in 1993 the Rafsanjani government "greatly increased its financial aid to Islamic political movements in Algeria, Bosnia, Lebanon, Pakistan, Tajikistan, and elsewhere in the world" (1993, 56). If Juergensmeyer is correct, it may seem contradictory that the Rafsanjani government, which had relaxed many of the Khomeini-era strictures inside Iran, would increase support for Islamic revolution elsewhere. This seeming contradiction, though, resembles the behavior of the post–Stalin Khrushchev and Brezhnev regimes, which also pursued a more relaxed policy internally while increasing support for revolution externally. Kenneth Katzman, however, has observed that it is the hard-line Revolutionary Guard in Iran that supports the export of revolution and that the Guard "is an autonomous, and not subordinate institution" over which the civilian government exercises influence but not control (1993, 135-39).

Also according to Katzman, in 1989 Iran extended its support beyond Shi'ite revolutionary groups to Sunni ones (1994).[5] Sudan has reportedly provided some degree of military assistance to Islamic revolutionary groups in Algeria, Tunisia, Egypt, Ethiopia, Chad, and Afghanistan (Juergensmeyer 1993, 48). Although Dr. Hasan Turabi of Sudan has denied that there is a military relationship between Khartoum and Tehran (1992, 56), the *New York Times* reported that Sudan serves as a transit point for Iranian arms going to Islamic revolutionaries in Algeria.[6] In addition, different Islamic revolutionary groups in Afghanistan have supplied arms and other assistance to Islamic revolutionaries fighting the unreformed Marxist-Leninists that are propped up by Russian and Uzbek forces in neighboring Tajikistan (Rubin 1994, 216-19). Soon after seizing Kabul in September 1996, the Taliban reportedly sent some of its fighters into Tajikistan to help the opposition there.[7]

REVOLUTIONARY IDEOLOGIES AND ASPIRING REVOLUTIONARIES

Why would the ideologies of successful revolutionaries in one country appeal to aspiring revolutionaries in others? Why in particular would aspiring revolutionaries seek to become part of a revolutionary wave led by another nation? The precise history of aspiring revolutionaries' becoming affiliated with the Marxist-Leninist, Arab nationalist, or Islamic fundamentalist revolutionary waves differs in each case. There are, however, some generalizations that can be made about how this process occurred.

To begin with, aspiring revolutionaries saw themselves fighting against the same or similar enemies as the central revolution. These aspiring revolutionaries were fighting not just their immediate enemy (the colonial power or the dictatorship), but the great power allies of those enemies. Sometimes this was literally true as when the United States intervened militarily in Vietnam and the USSR did so in Afghanistan. On other occasions, though, a great power might not significantly help its ally suppress the aspiring revolutionaries. But even when this was the case, the great power did not actively turn against its ally by aiding the revolutionaries.

Aspiring revolutionaries often received support from existing revolutionary regimes. In some cases, this amounted to substantial military aid over a period of years. In others, there may have been little or no actual military assistance, but a substantial degree of political and diplomatic support. This alone, however, was of great importance to the aspiring revolutionaries, especially since it was more than they received from the status quo powers. Even in those cases in which aspiring revolutionaries did not receive what they considered to be adequate levels of military or political support from the central revolution, there was always the hope that such assistance might be forthcoming.

Another reason for aspiring revolutionaries to affiliate with a revolutionary wave was competition from other revolutionary movements inside their country. Under circumstances where revolutionary movements could only operate with great difficulty, even limited external assistance from other revolutionary states would be an advantage. Of course, there were instances in which more than one revolutionary group sought recognition and assistance from a revolutionary wave. Before the departure of the Portuguese from Angola in 1975, both the MPLA and UNITA claimed to be Marxist-Leninist. The USSR and Cuba, however, chose to support the MPLA. The USSR's main rival within the Marxist-Leninist revolutionary wave—China—gave limited military assistance to all three opposition movements until shortly before Angola became formally independent (Porter 1984, 175-79).

But while any or all of these three motivations (sharing a common set of enemies, receiving assistance from revolutionary regimes, and rivalry with other aspiring revolutionary groups) may have encouraged aspiring revolutionaries to affiliate with a central revolution, they did not necessarily do so. Sharing a common set of enemies does not automatically lead to affiliation; it may only mean that a revolutionary movement in one country is part of the same "against" revolutionary wave as a central revolution. Nor does the receipt of military assistance from countries in a revolutionary wave guarantee that aspiring revolutionaries will affiliate with it after coming to power. In many cases, this issue has been moot since the aspiring revolutionaries have come to power quickly and unexpectedly through a coup d'etat. Nor does the fact that one group of aspiring revolutionaries claim affiliation with a revolutionary wave necessarily help it obtain assistance from a central revolution. On several occasions the USSR supported non-Marxist-Leninist revolutionary groups or regimes despite their hostility toward or suppression of Marxist-Leninist groups (Katz 1989, 58-76). The Marxist-Leninist revolutionary wave, however, is unique in this regard. There were no instances of Arab nationalist regimes favoring non-Arab nationalist revolutionaries over Arab nationalist ones. Nor have there been any instances in which Islamic revolutionary regimes have favored non-Islamic revolutionaries to Islamic ones.

The most basic motivation for aspiring revolutionaries anywhere to affiliate with a revolutionary wave is simply that they see it as a successful model. They regard the success of a revolutionary ideology elsewhere as providing a model for them to apply (in general if not specific terms) to their own country. Colburn described how the success of the Marxist-Leninist revolution in Russia inspired Mao Tse-tung, Fidel Castro, and Ho Chi Minh, and how the success of Marxist-Leninist revolution in China, Cuba, and Vietnam in turn inspired revolutionaries in other Third World countries (1994, 20-30). It was not so much 'Abd al-Nasir's seizure of power that inspired Arab nationalists in other countries as it was his apparent triumphs over "Western imperialism"—particularly the hasty withdrawal of British, French, and Israeli forces from the Suez Canal and Sinai Peninsula after their intervention there in 1956 (Hourani 1991, 405-07). With regard to the influence of the Iranian Revolution on the Arabs, Adeed Dawisha wrote, "Iran became the model and inspiration for radical Muslim activists in the Arab world" (1986, 117).

Unlike most other parts of the world, the Middle East is a region where aspiring revolutionaries have had a choice of revolutionary waves to affiliate with. And on occasion, rival revolutionary groups have risen up within the same nation and affiliated with different revolutionary waves.

Kerr relates how in Syria by 1958 members of the Arab nationalist Ba'th party and the Syrian Communist party had eliminated their rivals and then focused their attention on each other. The communists opposed the Ba'th party's desire to unite Syria with Egypt. Once unification took place in 1958, the Syrian Communists were eliminated as serious contenders for power (1971, 10-11).

In South Yemen, Arab nationalist FLOSY and Marxist-Leninist NLF revolutionary groups fought not only against the British, but against each other. When the British withdrew in 1967, the Marxist-Leninists were victorious (Katz 1986, 69-70).

Besides the Islamic fundamentalists, who eventually triumphed over all their opponents, there were several strands within the Iranian revolutionary movement, including Islamic democrats (such as Bani-Sadr), Marxist-Leninists (the Tudeh party), and the hybrid Islamic Marxists (the People's Mujahadin) (Bakhash 1984, chapter 9).

The Palestinian revolutionary movement has been divided among Arab nationalists (the PLO as well as smaller groups with links to particular Arab countries), Marxist-Leninists (the Popular Front for the Liberation of Palestine and the Democratic Front for the Liberation of Palestine), and, more recently, Islamic fundamentalists (Hamas and Islamic Jihad) (Adeed Dawisha 1986, 80-81; Legrain 1991, 71-74). While the Arab nationalist branch of the Palestinian revolutionary movement was able to prevent the Marxist-Leninist branch from dominating the movement, it is now facing a very serious challenge to its leadership from the relatively newer Islamic fundamentalist branch (Muslih 1995).

Revolutionary Waves and the "Legacy of Empire"

In addition to wanting to affiliate with revolutionary waves that aspiring revolutionaries see as models and possible sources of assistance, the "internationalist" aspect of a revolutionary wave's ideology has a particular advantage in many cases. Many of the countries where affiliate revolutions of all three varieties took place contain diverse ethnic, tribal, or religious groups that never voted democratically to live together as one nation. As in Russia and Iran, minority groups in many of the affiliate revolutionary countries are (or were historically) a majority within certain regions of the country.

This situation may have come about, as it did in China and Ethiopia, through the expansion of an indigenous empire. More frequently, however, it was the result of the European colonial powers drawing borders according to what they had been able to conquer, to negotiations among themselves, or simply to administrative convenience. In some cases, different groups (often hostile to each other) were included within one set of borders while a single group was split by them, as in many African countries. In Afghanistan, both processes were at work: the country took shape as an empire; although it was not successfully colonized, its borders were largely determined by Britain and Russia.

Aspiring revolutionaries did not create this "legacy of empire" of regionally dominant minorities in their countries. However, this problem affected them even before they came to power. In no case were aspiring revolutionaries actually willing to allow one or more regions of their country to secede, but preventing secession posed a problem. Aspiring revolutionaries could not use the same justification as the old regime ("divine right of kings" or "right of conquest"). This problem may also explain why many aspiring revolutionaries were so virulently opposed to liberal democracy, which separatists could use to insist on a plebiscite that would lead to secession. On the other hand, most aspiring revolutionaries did not want to alienate these regionally dominant minorities, but sought to win their support. While a narrowly nationalist ideology might well alienate them and spur them to pursue secession, an internationalist ideology such as Marxism-Leninism, Arab nationalism, or Islamic fundamentalism held the potential for uniting all (or most) of a country's diverse groups against the common enemy as well as providing a justification for keeping a country intact, no matter how arbitrarily or undemocratically its borders may have been drawn.

This problem of nations created by the legacy of empire that are not internally cohesive has been pervasive in the Marxist-Leninist revolutionary wave. In addition to Russia, with its many non-Russian nations, some of the East European countries that experienced subordinate revolutions suffered from a lack of internal cohesiveness dating from their independence decades earlier: Czechoslovakia (Czechs and Slovaks), Romania (with its large Hungarian population), and Bulgaria (with its large Turkish population). In addition, affiliate Marxist-Leninist revolutions took place in several countries with this problem. They were (in chronological order of occurrence): Yugoslavia (with its mixture of Serbs, Croats, Bosnian Muslims, Slovenians, Macedonians, Albanians, and others), Albania (where the

Albanians are divided between Gegs and Tosks), China (where the Chinese empire had acquired control over large non-Chinese areas including Tibet and Xinjiang), South Yemen (which was divided along tribal lines), Congo and Benin (which had both experienced regional rivalries), Ethiopia (consisting of Amharas, Tigrayans, Eritreans, Oromos, Western Somalis, and others), Guinea-Bissau (where there are five main tribal groups, plus others), Mozambique (with three main ethnic groups, plus others), Angola (with Mbundu and mesticoes in the middle, Ovimbundu in the south, and Bakongo in the north), and Afghanistan (with numerous ethnic groups including Pushtuns, Tajiks, Uzbeks, and Hazaras). In addition, while Nicaragua is a predominantly Hispanic country, it also contains a significant native American population on its Atlantic seaboard, which had not been integrated with the rest of the country before the Sandinista revolution.

This problem was present in all the countries in the Arab nationalist revolutionary wave. As was noted earlier, Egypt had a large Christian minority, though it was a minority throughout the country. Syria's population is predominantly Arab, but also contains Kurds. What is more, the Arab population is divided along religious lines; while the majority are Sunni Muslim, there are also Christians, 'Alawis, Druze, and Isma'ilis. In Iraq, Shi'ite Arabs constitute the majority population while Sunni Arabs and Kurds form large minorities. In addition to its Arab majority, Algeria contains a large Berber minority, concentrated in the Kabylia region in the northeast. North Yemen was divided both tribally (Hashid, Bakil, and others) and religiously (Zaydi Shi'ite and Shafi'i Sunni). In Sudan, there is a large non-Muslim population that predominates in the south. Libya is also divided tribally.

Lack of internal cohesion is also present in the Islamic revolutionary wave. The ethnic divisions of the three countries where Islamic revolution has actually occurred (Iran, Sudan, and Afghanistan) and several where Islamic revolutionary movements are active (Algeria, Syria, and Iraq) have already been described. The divisions existing in Lebanon, with its Christian, Sunni, Shi'ite, Druze, and other communities, are well known. In Tajikistan, the civil war between the former communists in power and the Islamic opposition also reflects regional divisions in this country. Saudi Arabia came into being when the rulers of one region (Najd) conquered the other three (al-Hasa, Hijaz, and Asir). In Oman, not only is the Dhofar province linguistically distinct and geographically separated from the rest of Oman by hundreds of miles of largely uninhabited desert, but the Omanis themselves are divided between Sunni and Ibadi Muslims. Finally, while it was not evident at the time 'Abd al-Nasir came to power in 1952, Mamoun Fandy has described how his and his successors' policies have led to the rise of an Islamic fundamentalist opposition movement, al-Jama'a al-Islamiyya, among Egypt's southerners (sa'idis), which is distinct from (and often at odds with) the northern-dominated Islamic fundamentalist opposition (1994).

Not all countries that are ethnically, religiously, or otherwise diverse become part of nondemocratic revolutionary waves. There are many such countries that have not, including India, which probably possesses the greatest degree of ethnic and religious diversity in any one country. Nor are countries that are not ethnically homogenous the only ones that join such revolutionary waves. Affiliate Marxist-Leninist revolutions did occur in countries with relatively homogenous populations in Cuba, Vietnam, Cambodia, and Grenada. What can be said, though, is that in many countries lacking cohesion as a result of the legacy of empire, aspiring revolutionaries saw the adoption of an internationalist revolutionary ideology and affiliation with a revolutionary wave as an effective means of uniting a diverse population and of justifying their country's continued territorial integrity.

SECESSIONIST MOVEMENTS AND REVOLUTIONARY WAVES

There have been occasions, however, when secessionist movements have adopted internationalist revolutionary ideologies. Part of their motivation for doing this was probably the hope of obtaining sympathy and support from a revolutionary wave. Such movements were largely unsuccessful not only in achieving secession, but in attracting much support from the revolutionary wave with which they attempted to affiliate.

A large number of secessionist movements attempted to affiliate themselves with the Marxist-Leninist revolutionary wave. In her painstaking research on Soviet support for revolutionary groups in Asia and Africa, Galia Golan showed that while Moscow often gave assistance to anticolonial or other movements operating within a country as a whole, it gave little or no support to groups seeking secession. Indeed, Moscow not only indicated its political opposition to many of these movements, but actually gave military assistance to governments (including non-Marxist ones) in order to suppress some of them. Moscow did give some support to Kurdish rebels seeking secession from Iraq and to Eritrean rebels seeking secession from Ethiopia, but in both cases Moscow switched to helping suppress these movements after pro-Soviet regimes came to power in Baghdad and Addis Ababa (Golan 1988, 262-65, 275-83).

There were only two regionally based rebel movements that Moscow especially supported: Bangladesh and Oman. In the case of Bangladesh, however, Moscow only supported its secession from Pakistan after India, the USSR's most important non-Marxist Third World ally, did so. In the case of Oman, Soviet support did not begin until the secessionist Dhofar Liberation Front (which began operations in 1965) was transformed into the Popular Front for the Liberation of the Occupied Arab Gulf (PFLOAG) under the aegis of the Marxist-Leninist regime that came to power in neighboring South Yemen in 1967. Instead of secession, PFLOAG's goal was to bring Marxist-Leninist revolution to all Oman as well as the other British-protected Arab Gulf monarchies (Golan 1988, 283-86). The one and only Marxist-Leninist secessionist movement that did succeed was in Eritrea, but this took place in 1993 after Moscow had ceased its support to Addis Ababa, the Marxist-Leninist regime in Ethiopia had been overthrown by an alliance led by Tigrayan and Eritrean rebels, and the Eritrean rebel movement had abandoned Marxism-Leninism. Eritrean secession, then, occurred not with the help of the Marxist-Leninist revolutionary wave, but in the wake of its collapse.

The ideology of Arab nationalism called for Arab unity. Arab nationalists, then, strongly opposed any effort to break up an existing Arab state, and did not consider any such movement to be within the Arab nationalist revolutionary wave. The most persistent secessionist movements in Arab countries have been those of non-Arabs in southern Sudan and in the Kurdish regions of Iraq. No secessionist effort in any Arab state has ever succeeded. On the other hand, most of the attempts at Arab unity among existing Arab states (which will be discussed later) have not succeeded either. Despite the artificiality of the borders that were drawn primarily by European colonial powers, the states they delimited have proven to be remarkably durable.

The Islamic revolutionary wave has had an ambivalent attitude toward secession. Islamic revolutionary regimes have opposed secession from predominantly Muslim states, especially by non-Muslims as in southern Sudan. They have not necessarily supported Muslim secessionist movements within Muslim states either. According to R. K. Ramazani, one of the reasons that Iran did not support the Kurdish rebellion in northern Iraq and the Shi'ite rebellion in southern Iraq in 1991 after Saddam Hussein's forces were expelled from Kuwait was for fear of how the breakup of Iraq might affect Iran itself (1992, 398). Munson has noted that Iranian radio broadcasts in Arabic have regularly exhorted the predominantly Shi'ite Arab population of al-Hasa (Saudi Arabia's so-called Eastern Province, where most of the Kingdom's oil reserves are located) to revolt. But the goal of the Shi'ite revolutionary organization that Iran has supported, the Organization of the Islamic Revolution in the Arab Peninsula, is (as its title suggests) not simply to break al-Hasa away from Saudi Arabia, but to overthrow the Saudi monarchy and come to power throughout the Kingdom as well as the other countries of the Arabian Peninsula (1988, 72-74).

On the other hand, the Islamic revolutionary wave has generally been supportive of revolutionary organizations in predominantly Muslim regions attempting to secede from non-Muslim countries. Muslim secessionist movements that have received political and even some degree of military support from Islamic revolutionary regimes include ones in Mindinao (from the Philippines), Kashmir (from India), Bosnia (from former Yugoslavia), and Chechnya (from Russia). The Islamic revolutionary wave, then, has exhibited a double standard concerning the legacy of empire, challenging it through support of Muslim efforts to secede from non-Muslim countries but defending it against non-Muslim and even Muslim efforts to secede from Muslim countries.

Differences Between Central Revolutions and Aspiring Revolutionaries

Despite their antipathy for a common enemy and fervor for a shared ideology, important differences can arise between aspiring revolutionaries on the one hand and central revolutions (as well as certain affiliate revolutions) on the other. These differences can arise when the revolution is a prolonged process in which a relationship has time to develop between aspiring revolutionaries and the central revolution. Of course, even when revolution occurs very quickly, as in a coup d'état, the aspiring revolutionaries may have contact with the central revolution beforehand—for example, via military officers who received training in a central revolutionary state and return home to lead a coup that gives birth to an affiliate revolution. But differences between aspiring revolutionaries and a central revolution, if they exist, are usually not apparent in such cases.

In cases where they are apparent, they have arisen over four different issues: 1) the level of assistance the aspiring revolutionaries receive; 2) differences in goals; 3) ideological differences; and 4) anticipated problems within a revolutionary wave if the aspiring revolutionaries succeed.

In cases where the revolutionary gestation period has been prolonged (such as in a protracted rural or urban revolution), aspiring revolutionaries have often sought military assistance from the central revolution and its affiliates. And often, the central revolution and its affiliates have indeed provided military assistance to aspiring revolutionaries, as was shown earlier. However, in many instances, the aspiring revolutionaries were not satisfied with the level of military assistance they received: they wanted more. In the Marxist-Leninist revolutionary wave, this was the case in several protracted revolutions, including those in China, North Vietnam, and South Yemen. This also occurred in Algeria—the one successful protracted revolution of the Arab nationalist wave. The Palestinians also bitterly resented what they considered to be the low level of military assistance they received from Arab nationalist states. It seems highly likely that various Islamic fundamentalist revolutionary groups, such as those in Tajikistan, have been disappointed over the low level of military assistance they have received from Iran.

Why have central revolutionary states not provided greater military assistance to aspiring revolutionaries whose success would expand the revolutionary wave? The answer to this question relates partly to the second set of differences: central revolutions and aspiring revolutionaries do not pursue the same goals. Aspiring revolutionaries have one overriding focus: coming to power. A central revolutionary state, however, has many goals. It wants the revolutionary wave to expand. But it also wants (usually) to avoid war with the status quo powers. A strong degree of involvement in support of revolutionaries whose enemy government is strongly supported by the status quo powers risks a broader confrontation that central revolutionary states usually seek to avoid. During the late 1950s and early 1960s, when China vociferously criticized the USSR for what Mao judged to be its insufficient support to the "national liberation movement" in the Third World, Soviet leader Khrushchev justified restraint in this regard by arguing that local wars involving the nuclear powers could escalate into world war that would destroy socialism as well as capitalism (Katz 1982, 18-19).

Even when support to aspiring revolutionaries did not seriously risk war for the central revolutionary state, the state might be reluctant to provide much aid if it sought cooperative relations with the status quo powers. Of course, central revolutionary states have sometimes acted as if they "can have their cake and eat it too." During the 1970s, for example, the Soviet leadership seemed to believe that it could increase Moscow's military involvement in the Third World without jeopardizing progress on arms control and detente with the United States (Katz 1989).

But even when the central revolution was not seeking cooperative relations with the status quo great powers, it might be seeking an alliance with regional states outside their revolutionary wave, such as when the USSR hoped to woo non-Marxist Third World states away from the West or when Iran cooperated with Syria against their common foe, Iraq. Support for aspiring revolutionaries fighting against these governments would have been incompatible with cooperating with them.

The general lack of support by central revolutions for aspiring secessionist revolutionaries can be understood in this context. Central revolutionary states have not been enthusiastic about supporting a principle that most other states (including revolutionary ones) do not wish to see applied to themselves.

Central revolutions and aspiring revolutionaries could also be divided by disagreements about ideology. This might occur because the aspiring revolutionaries adopted the ideology of a rival revolution that denounced the central revolution. The New People's Army in the Philippines and Sendero Luminoso in Peru, for example, proclaimed themselves to be Maoist, and were anti-Soviet as well as anti-American. Precisely why they chose to be Maoist is unclear. Although they did not receive any assistance from the USSR (which, in fact, sought good relations with the non-Marxist governments in both countries), they did not receive any from China either. The heyday of their guerrilla activity (the mid-1980s for the New People's Army and the late 1980s/early 1990s for Sendero Luminoso) occurred long after China had ceased its efforts to export revolution and wrest from Moscow the position of acknowledged leader of the world communist movement. Part of their preference for Maoism may have been a desire to distinguish themselves from what they (accurately) considered to be unrevolutionary pro-Soviet Marxist-Leninist parties. But basically, their Maoism seems to have been the result of the guerrilla leaderships' (false) perception of its utility in organizing rural revolution, despite their knowledge of its abandonment by China.

The Egyptian Muslim Brotherhood, as well as other aspiring Sunni revolutionaries, have some serious ideological differences with Iranian Shi'ite fundamentalism. One of the most important differences is that Sunni fundamentalists reject the central tenet of Ayatollah Khomeini's concept of Islamic governance: the guardianship of the jurisconsult *(vilayat-i faqih)*, who is a top-ranking cleric with the power to reject or overturn the decisions of elected officials, including the president and the parliament. Unlike in Iran—where the leadership of the Islamic revolutionaries, and later the regime, came from the ranks of the Shi'ite clerics—aspiring Sunni revolutionary groups tend to be led by laymen. According to Ayubi, because Sunni clerics are generally unrevolutionary, "Islamic movements in Sunni societies . . . show signs of becoming increasingly anti-clerical" (1991, 155). This ideological difference has important implications: lay revolutionaries who do not defer to the clergy before coming to power are unlikely to defer to clerics either from their own country or from another one such as Iran afterward.

A particularly sensitive point of ideological disagreement can be over the revolutionary model espoused by the central revolutionary state. Instead of seeing how they came to power as resulting from the peculiar circumstances of their own country, successful revolutionaries often hold up the path they took as the model to be followed by all other aspiring revolutionaries within their revolutionary wave. But when aspiring revolutionaries have attempted to replicate this revolutionary model (sometimes under the direct tutelage of the regime advocating it), the model has failed. This occurred in a spectacular manner in China during the 1920s. Following Moscow's advice, the Chinese Communist party staged uprisings that helped the Kuomintang capture key cities, but was immediately attacked by the Kuomintang afterward. Following Moscow's advice again, the weakened Chinese Communist party attempted to stage an urban revolutionary uprising against the Kuomintang, but was again defeated by it (Ulam 1974, 170-81).

How do aspiring revolutionaries react when they lose faith in the revolutionary model advocated by the central revolution? In China, Mao Tsetung jettisoned the model of urban revolution advanced by Moscow and developed a model of rural revolution that he (correctly) thought was more appropriate to Chinese circumstances. Fidel Castro not only rejected the Soviet model of urban revolution for Cuba, but modified the Chinese model of rural revolution by subtracting the role of his country's existing Communist party (which Castro considered to be unrevolutionary) from it. Ironically, while Castro rejected the appropriateness of other successful Marxist-Leninist revolutionary models for Cuba, he saw the Cuban Revolution as a model for the rest of Latin America. Aggressive Cuban efforts to export this model to other Latin American countries, however, failed in the mid-1960s (Katz 1983).

Ideological differences in general, and differences about revolutionary methodology in particular, are important because they relate to the fourth difference between central revolutions and aspiring revolutionaries: anticipated problems within a revolutionary wave if aspiring revolutionaries succeed in coming to power. If aspiring revolutionaries disagree with a central revolution on ideological matters even before they come to power and are still dependent on it for help, the central revolutionary leadership has good reason to wonder how these aspiring revolutionaries will behave after they succeed, especially if they are then less dependent. Through advocating an alternative revolutionary methodology, the affiliate revolutionaries are essentially saying that the one espoused by the central revolution is not applicable in certain areas of the world, is no longer applicable due to changed circumstances, or both. The central revolution, then, may see the advocacy of an alternative revolutionary methodology by aspiring revolutionaries as especially threatening since it fears a challenge to its leadership within the revolutionary wave.

What can the central revolution do under such circumstances? There are basically two strategies it can pursue: 1) support the aspiring revolutionaries despite their ideological heterodoxy in the belief that their victory will strengthen the revolutionary wave vis-à-vis the status quo powers and that ideological differences can be smoothed over; or 2) deny or limit support to the aspiring revolutionaries in order to prevent them coming to power, since their victory is seen by the central revolution to be harmful to its interests. The problem with the first strategy is that it might not work: serious differences between the central revolution and aspiring revolutionaries may persist and become more complicated after the latter come to power. The second strategy avoids this risk altogether—if, that is, the strategy succeeds and the obstreperous aspiring revolutionaries do not come to power. But if the obstreperous aspiring revolutionaries actually do come to power despite the lack of assistance from the central revolution, the relationship between them and the central revolution is likely to be highly problematic.

In the Marxist-Leninist revolutionary wave, the USSR pursued both strategies, though at different times. As was discussed earlier, Stalin tried to persuade Mao Tse-tung to discontinue his revolution from 1945 to 1947, and to not press for control of all China in 1948. Especially after the breakdown of Soviet-Yugoslav relations in 1948, Stalin understood that an independent Marxist-Leninist guerrilla leader could avoid control from Moscow. And Mao's defiance of Stalin in the late 1940s before he came to power was indeed a precursor to his more formidable challenge to Moscow's leadership of the Marxist-Leninist revolutionary wave later. On the other hand, Khrushchev and Brezhnev pursued the more tolerant strategy of supporting a heterodox group of aspiring revolutionaries (both Marxist-Leninist and non-Marxist-Leninist) in many Third World countries. This strategy met with mixed results: some aspiring revolutionaries affiliated closely with the USSR after coming to power while others kept it at arms length (MacFarlane 1990).

In the Arab nationalist revolutionary wave, there was little opportunity for differences to develop between the central revolution and aspiring revolutionaries since almost all of these revolutions occurred very quickly via coups d'etat. In Algeria, the one protracted Arab nationalist revolution that succeeded, there were no significant ideological differences between the aspiring revolutionaries and Egypt.

In the Islamic revolutionary wave, there is evidence that Iran has also pursued both strategies. After its initial failure to promote Shi'ite Islamic revolution, Iran expanded its support to Sunni Islamic revolutionaries in the late 1980s. Tehran apparently decided that the victory of these groups would benefit Iranian interests despite its ideological differences with them. But while Iran has been willing to tolerate ideological differences with Sunni revolutionaries, there is evidence that it is unwilling to tolerate them with Shi'ite ones. Said Amir Arjomand has suggested that one of the reasons Iran did not support the 1991 Shi'ite revolt in Iraq was because of Grand Ayatollah Abu'l-Qasim Khoi's leading role in it: "Khoi, the highest Shi'ite religious leader *(marja' al-taqlid)* in Iraq, had been Khomeini's chief rival; pictures of Khoi were burned during the Iranian Revolution" (Arjomand 1991, 64). Whereas aspiring Sunni revolutionaries who come to power pose little threat to the Iranian clergy's leadership of the Shi'ite revolutionary movement, successful Shi'ite revolutionaries in Iraq who oppose the Iranian clergy might. Whether a successful Shi'ite Islamic fundamentalist revolution in Iraq in 1991 actually would have posed a leadership challenge to Iran the way Mao did to the USSR, however, cannot be known since Saddam Hussein was able to quickly crush it.

Yet despite the many differences that arise between central revolutions and aspiring revolutionaries, the two are usually allied to each other at the point when aspiring revolutionaries actually come to power. This was not always the case, however, as with the Taliban which, due to its strongly anti-Shi'ite position, had developed poor relations with Iran before it captured most of Afghanistan in 1996 (Barfield 1996, 42). Usually, though, aspiring revolutionaries who broke with the central revolution did not come to power. The fact that they did this and so cut themselves off from whatever assistance they could have received from the central revolution may have been part of the reason for their failure. It is after aspiring revolutionary movements become affiliate revolutions that their differences with the central revolution (as well as other affiliate revolutions) some times reach the breaking point. But in some cases, even where there was much bad feeling between the new affiliate revolution and the central revolution, it took years for this point to be reached, though in others it was reached in a matter of days. And when this point is reached, one of the most divisive issues in their relationship is how the central revolution treated the affiliate revolutionaries before they came to power.

THE ISLAMIC FUNDAMENTALIST WAVE: PROSPECTS FOR FURTHER EXPANSION

What is the likelihood that the Islamic fundamentalist revolutionary wave will expand to other countries? Aspiring Islamic fundamentalist revolutionaries now are strong enough to sustain protracted insurgency against the governments of Algeria, Egypt, and Tajikistan. Significant Islamic fundamentalist revolutionary movements also exist in Tunisia, Saudi Arabia, Oman, Bahrain, Iraq, and elsewhere. Aspiring Islamic fundamentalist revolutionaries may well be prevented from coming to power in many of these cases, just as aspiring Marxist-Leninist and Arab nationalist revolutionaries were prevented from coming to power in many countries where they were active. But previous experience suggests that it will be difficult to prevent them from coming to power in all cases.

Most of the governments against which aspiring Islamic fundamentalist revolutionaries are currently active possess many of the general characteristics of other governments that previously succumbed to aspiring revolutionaries from the Marxist-Leninist, Arab nationalist, and Islamic fundamentalist revolutions in the past. They are mainly nondemocratic governments that so far have not exhibited any serious interest in democratization, and have sought to crush their democratic as well as their nondemocratic opponents. All (including oil-rich but increasingly cash-poor and indebted Saudi Arabia) are facing economic crises to a greater or lesser extent. Many are experiencing military stalemates in the form of their inability to defeat protracted insurgencies against them (Algeria, Egypt, and Tajikistan), sporadic rebellion from a variety of internal opponents (Iraq), or extraordinarily high defense expenditures, despite severe economic constraints, for fear of potential internal and external opponents (Saudi Arabia and Oman). In addition, while popular support for the aspiring Islamic fundamentalists fighting against them may not necessarily be strong, all these regimes appear to have lost whatever popular support they may once have enjoyed (if they ever did). They remain in power through the use of force. And all of them except Iraq receive significant military support from one or more of the major status quo powers (France vis-à-vis North Africa, the U.S. vis-à-vis Egypt and the Arabian Peninsula, and Russia vis-à-vis Central Asia).

Just because these regimes are experiencing these problems, however, does not mean that they will inevitably succumb to Islamic fundamentalist revolution. But if the crises they are experiencing escalate (as they already have in Algeria and Tajikistan), the major status quo powers will face serious problems in attempting to defend them. There are important domestic constraints on their ability to employ their own armed forces to defend their embattled status quo (or revolutionary-turned–status quo) allies. While the American public was willing to send ground forces to Saudi Arabia to protect the Kingdom against an external threat from Iraq, it is highly doubtful that it would long tolerate doing so to protect either Saudi Arabia or Egypt (its two main allies in the region) against their internal opponents. Similarly, as much as French public opinion appears to fear the success of Islamic fundamentalist revolution in Algeria, it does not appear willing to send its forces to fight another war in that country. Post-Soviet Russia (which, notwithstanding whether or not it is democratic, is definitely one of the major status quo powers seeking to halt the expansion of the Islamic fundamentalist wave) has since 1992 used its armed forces to prop up the postrevolutionary, nondemocratic Marxist-Leninist regime in Tajikistan against its opponents—some of whom are aspiring Islamic fundamentalist revolutionaries. However, this war—in which Moscow and its allies appear to be losing ground to the opposition—is not popular with the Russian public.[8] Further, the Tajik opposition could only have been heartened by the August 1996 Russian-Chechen cease-fire agreement, which called for the withdrawal of Russian troops from Chechnya and the effective secession of control over the region to the Chechen opposition forces that Moscow had been fighting ineffectually since late 1994. For if Russia was unwilling to sustain a conflict against Muslim opposition forces in a region inside the Russian Federation, it is not likely to be willing or able to sustain one against similar forces outside of it.

But if there are severe limits on the extent to which the major status quo powers can directly intervene to protect their embattled status quo allies, there remains the tried-and-true method of arms transfers. As previous experience has shown, however, this is hardly an infallible method of defeating aspiring revolutionaries. Public opinion in the major Western powers can also limit the extent to which these governments can transfer arms to their embattled allies. The perception that it is being abandoned or not strongly supported can serve to undercut embattled allies as well as embolden aspiring revolutionaries. On the other hand, large-scale arms transfers to an embattled ally will be of little use if its armed forces cannot or will not use them effectively. They can even be counterproductive if elements within the armed forces receiving them are aspiring revolutionaries themselves.

An alternative to military support for nondemocratic regimes is Western support for democratization in them. It is argued that if the citizens of these countries had the opportunity to vote dictatorial regimes out of office, nondemocratic opposition movements would receive far fewer votes than democratic ones.[9] In predominantly Muslim countries the democratic elements within Islamic opposition movements would prove to be more popular and hence stronger than the nondemocratic ones, as appeared to be the case in Algeria before the FIS was prevented from achieving the parliamentary majority it was about to receive before elections were canceled.[10]

The prospect of replacing a nondemocratic status quo regime and preempting the rise of a nondemocratic Islamic fundamentalist revolutionary one all at once through promoting the emergence of democracy is highly appealing. The United States has even had some success in promoting democratization in several nondemocratic status quo regimes allied to it, such as the Philippines, South Korea, and Chile. There are, however, several important obstacles to replicating this experience in Muslim countries where Islamic fundamentalist revolutionaries are active.

Where status quo nondemocratic regimes are opposed to democratization, democracy is obstructed—though not insurmountably, as the Philippine, South Korean, and Chilean cases demonstrated. But in these three cases, there was relatively little risk for the United States since the democratic opposition forces were relatively strong while the nondemocratic ones were relatively weak (if existent) and were not receiving external support from a nondemocratic revolutionary wave.

These conditions are not present in the Muslim countries where aspiring Islamic fundamentalist revolutionaries are now active. Even where nondemocratic opposition forces do not appear to be strong, democratic ones do not appear to be strong either. But whatever their relative strength vis-à-vis each other, the major status quo powers are subject to the fear that any attempt at democratization will only be taken advantage of by the aspiring Islamic fundamentalist revolutionaries to come to power; destroy democracy; and join Iran, Sudan, and the rest of the Islamic fundamentalist wave in exporting revolution to other countries.[11] Whether or not this fear is justified, the embattled status quo regimes espouse this argument vociferously in order to avoid pressure to relinquish power through democratization. The governments of the major Western powers often accept it also, since, as John Esposito put it, "democracy raises the prospect of old and reliable friends or client states being transformed into more independent and less predictable nations which might make Western access to their oil less secure" (1992, 185).

The problem with this argument, however, is that it can become a self-fulfilling prophecy. Nondemocratic status quo governments in the Muslim world and the aspiring Islamic fundamentalist revolutionaries opposed to them have one goal in common: both oppose the rise of democratic Islamic opposition groups. Facing two opponents who do not hesitate to use force against them and receiving no external support themselves, democratic Islamic opposition movements can be successfully suppressed. But if this happens and the unpopular status quo government—the focus of popular discontent—also experiences a regime crisis, it is the nondemocratic opposition that is then in a strong position to seize power. And at this point, it has no need to defer to the weak democratic opposition.

It is possible, of course, that embattled status quo regimes can defeat aspiring Islamic fundamentalist revolutionaries by military means. But, as previous experience has shown, such efforts can fail. It is also possible that aspiring Islamic fundamentalist revolutionaries could take advantage of free elections to come to power and then destroy democracy. But it is not inevitable that they will be able to do this. However, in those cases where the major status quo powers are unwilling or unable either to keep their embattled nondemocratic allies in power by military means or to promote democratization as an alternative to the two nondemocratic antagonists, then there are strong prospects for the eventual seizure of power by aspiring nondemocratic Islamic fundamentalist revolutionaries.

Chapter 3

The Central Revolution
and Affiliate Revolutions

Once aspiring revolutionaries succeed in coming to power, the regime they create in emulation of the central revolution usually becomes an affiliate revolution within its particular revolutionary wave. But how long does the alliance between the central revolution and an affiliate revolution last? In some cases, as with the USSR and Cuba, the alliance lasts for decades. In others, the alliance lasts a few years, but ends in mutual antagonism, as it did between the USSR and China. In others still, the alliance can be so loose that it is essentially meaningless. And in still other cases, the new "affiliate" revolutionary regime immediately disaffiliates itself from the central revolution and its other affiliates, as did the revolutionary regime that overthrew the monarchy in Iraq vis-à-vis the United Arab Republic in 1958, and the Khmer Rouge vis-à-vis Hanoi and Moscow in 1975.

This chapter will first briefly describe the relationships that have existed between central revolutions and affiliate revolutions in the three revolutionary waves. It will then analyze the reasons why disaffiliation occurs in some cases and affiliation persists in others. Whether the patterns of affiliation and disaffiliation that emerged in the Marxist-Leninist, Arab nationalist, or so far in the Islamic fundamentalist revolutionary waves will persist in an expanded Islamic fundamentalist revolutionary wave will then be examined.

THE HISTORICAL RECORD

In the Marxist-Leninist revolutionary wave, the character and length of Marxist-Leninist revolutionary regimes' affiliation with the USSR was highly varied. Not surprisingly, the Marxist-Leninist regimes established by subordinate revolutions (revolutions from without brought to other countries by invading Soviet forces) in Mongolia, Poland, East Germany, Czechoslovakia, Hungary, and Bulgaria remained subordinate to the USSR from the time they occurred (1920 in Mongolia, the end of World War II in Eastern Europe) until 1989, when Mikhail Gorbachev signalled that the USSR was no longer willing to use force to maintain the Marxist-Leninist revolutionary wave. Two Marxist-Leninist revolutionary regimes established by Soviet forces, however, were able to escape their subordinate status: North Korea and Romania. North Korea took advantage of the Sino-Soviet rift that developed in the late 1950s and early 1960s to end its subordination to the USSR, and it managed to affiliate itself with both Moscow and Beijing even though they were hostile toward each other (Rubinstein 1992, 169-71). By the mid-1960s, Romania also had managed to distance itself from the USSR, with which it frequently expressed differences on foreign policy issues. Yet while Romania sometimes appeared to be disaffiliated from the USSR, from the mid-1960s it might more accurately be described as an involuntary affiliate or an insubordinate subordinate, but not as strictly subordinate to Moscow as Poland, East Germany, Czechoslovakia, and Hungary (Zimmerman 1984, 133-36).

In both North Korea and Romania, an end to their strictly subordinate relationships vis-à-vis the USSR came about after the departure of Soviet troops from these countries. Poland, East Germany, Czechoslovakia, and Hungary remained subordinate to the USSR by the presence of Soviet troops, though Moscow had to either threaten the use of force (Poland 1956 and 1981) or actually use it (East Germany 1953, Hungary 1956, and Czechoslovakia 1968). Bulgaria was the one East European country in which, after Stalin, the USSR did not keep its troops stationed but which remained subordinate to the USSR anyway (Johnson 1984). This anomaly might be best explained by the fact that the Bulgarians feared their neighbors (including other Marxist-Leninist ones), genuinely looked to Moscow as their protector, and had no illusions about their ability to sustain a disaffiliated or unaffiliated Marxist-Leninist regime independent of the USSR. After Stalin, then, Bulgaria's relationship with the USSR evolved from being strictly subordinate to being what might be called voluntarily subordinate.

The affiliate Marxist-Leninist regimes that arose at the end of World War II in Yugoslavia and Albania both experienced dramatic change in their relations with the USSR. Tito's regime in Yugoslavia was closely and enthusiastically affiliated with Moscow from the time it came to power in 1944 until early 1948 when Stalin, seeking greater Soviet control over the country, sought to oust Tito and replace him with a more pro-Soviet leadership. Stalin's plan backfired; not only did Tito remain firmly in control of Yugoslavia, but he quickly disaffiliated his regime from the USSR. Yugoslavia remained a disaffiliated member of the Marxist-Leninist revolutionary wave until both the wave and Yugoslavia ceased to exist (Zimmerman 1984, 128-33). Ironically, Russia and what remains of Yugoslavia under Serbian control became affiliated with each other once again in the early 1990s, but not on the basis of shared adherence to Marxism-Leninism (Lynch and Lukic 1993).

From its emergence in 1944 until the Soviet-Yugoslav rift in 1948, the Marxist regime in Albania was closely affiliated with Yugoslavia, and by implication with the USSR. Resenting Yugoslav influence in their country, the Albanian leadership took advantage of the Soviet-Yugoslav rift to affiliate with the USSR and disaffiliate with Yugoslavia in 1948. Later, during the Khrushchev years, the Albanian leadership feared the possibility of a Soviet-Yugoslav rapprochement in which Albania's interests would be sacrificed, and so seized upon the growing Sino-Soviet rift to affiliate with China and disaffiliate with the USSR in 1960. Albania remained affiliated with China until 1978, when Beijing and Washington established diplomatic relations, at which point the regime in Albania became completely disaffiliated until its demise in 1991-92 (Jelavich 1983, 331-33, 378-84).

Despite Mao Tse-tung's serious differences with Stalin beforehand, the Marxist-Leninist regime that came to power in China in 1949 became closely affiliated with the USSR. Stalin died in 1953, and Mao Tse-tung launched his bid for the leadership of the Marxist-Leninist revolutionary wave in the mid-1950s. China, then, became a rival revolution to the USSR, and supported Marxist revolutionaries elsewhere in competition with Moscow. By the time Mao died in 1976, however, China had ceased its efforts to rival Moscow for the leadership of the revolutionary wave and became simply a disaffiliated revolution (Rubinstein 1992, 151-61). With the downfall of the Marxist-Leninist regime in the USSR in 1991, and the general collapse of the revolutionary wave, China might now be described as an unaffiliated—and unrevolutionary—Marxist-Leninist regime.

With the withdrawal of the French from Indochina in 1954, the Marxist-Leninist regime in North Vietnam became affiliated with both the USSR and China, which were then still allies. Like North Korea, North Vietnam remained affiliated with both the USSR and China, despite the Sino-Soviet rift, in order to maintain a degree of independence from both. With the spread of Marxist-Leninist revolution to the rest of Indochina in 1975, South Vietnam came under the direct control of the North, and a regime largely subordinate to Hanoi was established in Laos. The Khmer Rouge regime that emerged in Cambodia, however, immediately disaffiliated from Hanoi, as well as Moscow, and affiliated with China instead. By the end of 1978, Vietnam and China had become completely disaffiliated with each other, while Vietnam became closely affiliated with the USSR. After the Vietnamese invasion of Cambodia that year, Cambodia switched from being affiliated with China to being subordinate to Vietnam (Pike 1987, 180-214). The situation changed again, though, in 1989 when Vietnamese forces were withdrawn from Cambodia. Since then, Cambodia has derevolutionized (though China's affiliate, the Khmer Rouge, had not given up its efforts to regain power), while the Marxist-Leninist regimes in Vietnam and Laos have, like the one in China, become unrevolutionary (Dommen 1995; Goodman 1995; Um 1995).

After coming to power in 1959, the Marxist-Leninist regime in Cuba soon affiliated itself with the USSR (a move that was really only accepted by Moscow in 1961). Cuba remained closely affiliated with the USSR until the collapse of communism in 1991. At one point in the mid-1960s, however, Cuba seemed to be acting as a rival to the USSR when the two backed opposing Marxist-Leninist revolutionary groups with very different strategies in other Latin American countries. However, after Cuba's attempt to export revolution without Moscow's blessing collapsed in 1967, Havana gave up these efforts and reverted to being a filial affiliate. In the mid-1970s, though, Havana would revive its efforts to export revolution, but would do so with Moscow's blessing (Katz 1983, 93-98).

The Marxist-Leninist regime that came to power in South Yemen in 1967 was at first only loosely affiliated with both the USSR and China not so much in an effort to maintain its independence from them but as a result of the party leadership's being split between pro-Soviet and pro-Chinese wings. The rivalry between the two wings came to a head in 1978 when the pro-Soviet wing ousted (and executed) the pro-Chinese leader. South Yemen then became closely affiliated with Moscow from 1978 until 1990 when, as the Marxist-Leninist revolutionary wave was collapsing,

South Yemen merged with Arab nationalist (and much more populous) North Yemen (Katz 1986, 90-95; Dunbar 1992, 463-65).

There were eight Marxist-Leninist revolutions in Africa during the 1970s. Five of them (the Congo, 1964 and 1968; Benin, 1972; Guinea-Bissau, 1974; Cape Verde, 1975; and Madagascar, 1975) became only loosely affiliated with the USSR at the time of their revolutions. With the passage of time, their affiliation attenuated even further, to the point where they really were unaffiliated Marxist-Leninist regimes (Fukuyama 1985, 125; *Africa South of the Sahara* 1994, 152-53, 235-36, 289-90, 441, 509-11). However, two other Marxist-Leninist revolutions (Ethiopia, 1974; and Angola, 1975) were closely affiliated with the USSR and Cuba from the time their revolutions succeeded until the Marxist-Leninist revolutionary wave collapsed (MacFarlane 1992; Remnek 1993). After the withdrawal of Soviet and Cuban military assistance, the Marxist-Leninist regime in Ethiopia collapsed while the one in Angola became bogged down in civil war (Marcum 1993; *Africa South of the Sahara* 1994, 355-56). The eighth African Marxist-Leninist regime, Mozambique, became more closely affiliated with the USSR than the first five but less so than Ethiopia and Angola. After the collapse of the Marxist-Leninist revolutionary wave, its ruling party was able to negotiate (with UN mediation) an end to its civil war and to win the elections that were held afterward (Rubinstein 1988, 215-16; Lloyd 1995).

The regime that seized power in Afghanistan in April 1978 was closely affiliated with the USSR until the Soviet invasion of Afghanistan in December 1979 when the regime in Kabul became subordinate to Moscow. It remained subordinate to the USSR until the completion of the Soviet withdrawal from Afghanistan in February 1989, at which point the regime in Kabul once again became affiliated with Moscow. It retained this status until the Marxist-Leninist regime was overthrown by Islamic revolutionary forces in 1992 (Rais 1992; *Strategic Survey 1992-1993*, 175-77).

The last two Marxist-Leninist revolutions occurred in Grenada and Nicaragua in 1979. The two became closely affiliated with Cuba and the USSR. Grenada's affiliation with them lasted until 1983 when an American-led military intervention ousted the Marxist-Leninist regime and undertook a democratic revolution from without (Valenta and Valenta 1986). Nicaragua's affiliation lasted until 1990 when, as the Marxist-Leninist revolutionary wave was collapsing, the ruling Sandinistas accepted their defeat in the elections that year (Rodman 1994, 222-56, 400-50).

The Arab nationalist revolutionary wave also had a varied record on character and length of affiliation. One of the most dramatic examples of affiliation among kindred revolutions was the decision by the Ba'th party of Syria to merge in 1958 into the United Arab Republic under the leadership of Egypt's 'Abd al-Nasir. This affiliation, however, came to an equally dramatic end in 1961 when Syria disaffiliated with Egypt by seceding from the UAR. Egypt, Syria, and Iraq attempted to negotiate another merger in 1963, but this effort failed (Kerr 1971, 11-25).

Malcolm Kerr described how the July 1958 Arab nationalist revolution in Iraq first affiliated with and then almost immediately disaffiliated with Egypt:

> 'Abd al-Nasir's picture suddenly blossomed forth in Baghdad shop windows on 14 July; then almost as quickly it disappeared. . . . The leading Arab nationalist figure, Colonel 'Abd al-Salam 'Arif, two days after the revolution stood on a balcony in Damascus with . . . 'Abd al-Nasir to receive the cheers of the crowd . . . By the end of the year relations between Iraq and the UAR were even worse than they had been in the days of the old regime" (1971, 17).

In addition to the failed effort to merge with Egypt and Syria in 1963, the 1964 announcement that Iraq and Egypt had agreed to merge over a two-year period also came to nothing (Kerr 1971, 123).

Syria and Iraq did not just disaffiliate with Egypt, but attempted to rival it (and each other). Although both Syrian and Iraqi Ba'th party cells were established in other countries, no other successful Arab nationalist revolution acknowledged Syria or Iraq as a central revolution or affiliated with either of them as such. Iraq under Saddam Hussein would attempt to create subordinate revolutions in Khuzistan (the predominantly Arab region of southwestern Iran bordering Iraq) in 1980 and in Kuwait in 1990 (al-Khalil 1989, 266-70; Bishku 1991). These efforts, however, were reversed by Iran and an American-led UN coalition, respectively. Between 1975 and 1991, Syria gained control over much of Lebanon. But instead of having created a subordinate Arab nationalist regime resembling its own, Syria has become the main arbiter within the existing system of contending communities in Lebanon (Hourani 1991, 430-32).

The Arab nationalist regime that came to power in North Yemen in 1962 was very closely affiliated with Egypt until the end of 1967. Since the Egyptian forces in North Yemen outnumbered the Yemeni republican forces (whom they were there to protect) by as much as ten to one, North Yemen might more accurately be described as a subordinate revolution during this period. This status changed, however, when 'Abd al-Nasir decided to withdraw his troops from North Yemen in 1967. Royalist forces surrounded the capital, and it was widely expected that the Arab nationalist regime in North Yemen would collapse. But the North Yemeni revolutionary regime survived, albeit with a different leadership, which was no longer affiliated with Egypt (Stookey 1978, 225-49; Katz 1986, 20-21). Unlike Syria and Iraq, which disaffiliated with Cairo and became rivals to it, North Yemen became an unaffiliated Arab nationalist regime after the Egyptian withdrawal. In 1990, Arab nationalist North Yemen and formerly Marxist-Leninist South Yemen would merge into a single nation dominated by the leadership of the more populous North. A civil war broke out in 1994 during which the southern leadership attempted to recreate an independent South Yemen, but this effort was defeated and Yemen has remained united (Hudson 1995).

The revolutionary regimes that came to power in Algeria in 1962 and Sudan in 1969 did not closely affiliate with Egypt or any other Arab nationalist revolution, nor did they attempt to rival any of these for the leadership of the revolutionary wave as a whole. Algeria and Sudan, then, could best be described as unaffiliated Arab nationalist revolutions. By contrast, the revolutionary regime that came to power in Libya in 1969 did seek to lead the Arab nationalist revolutionary wave. Albert Hourani described the goal of Libya's leader, Mu'ammar al-Qadhafi, as "trying to take up the mantle of 'Abd al-Nasir, without any basis of strength except what money could provide" (1991, 428). Libya, however, did not so much attempt to rival Egypt as to replace it as the central revolution after Cairo abandoned this role following its defeat in the 1967 Arab-Israeli war and the death of 'Abd al-Nasir in 1970. In an effort to build a pan-Arab state akin to the UAR, Libya signed separate unity agreements with Egypt, Sudan, Tunisia, and Morocco. None of these projects, however, came to fruition. Al-Qadhafi attempted to establish a revolution in Chad that would be subordinate to his own, but although Libya came to control the northern half of the country, this effort was defeated by both Chadian and French armed forces (Deeb 1989).

There has also been variation in the extent to which the few other Islamic fundamentalist revolutions that have occurred have affiliated with Iran. Since it came to power in 1989, the Islamic revolutionary regime in Sudan has affiliated closely with Tehran. The two governments have cooperated in providing training and support to aspiring

Islamic revolutionaries in other countries (Katzman 1993, 100, 177; Cordesman 1994, 34-35). By contrast, the Sunni fundamentalist forces that ousted Afghanistan's Marxist-Leninist regime in 1992 were largely unaffiliated with Iran. Indeed, there was even a degree of tension between them and Tehran over Tehran's support for the Shi'ite minority in Afghanistan (Dorronsoro 1995). This first Afghan Islamic fundamentalist regime, however, drew closer to Tehran as the anti-Shi'ite Taliban gained strength and drove it from the capital into the northern part of the country in 1996.[1]

There was little affiliation between Iran and the Islamic/democratic coalition that ruled Tajikistan for a few months in 1992 before the Soviet regime it ousted was restored by Russian and Uzbek forces (Panico 1993; Katz 1995a, 255). Since then, however, the aspiring—or reaspiring—Tajik revolutionaries and Tehran have reportedly established a closer affiliation (Cordesman 1994, 35). This, however, has probably attenuated as Iran has improved its relations with both Russia and the ex-communist regime in Tajikistan while the Tajik opposition has allegedly received some degree of support from the anti-Iranian Taliban in Afghanistan (Katz 1995-96).[2]

DISAFFILIATION

Disaffiliation generally occurs throughout revolutionary waves as they collapse. This process, however, will not be discussed here but in the next chapter. This section of this chapter will analyze the conditions under which disaffiliation, or lack of strong affiliation, occurs while a revolutionary wave is in operation.

There were eighteen affiliate revolutions within the Marxist-Leninist revolutionary wave. Of these, four—Yugoslavia, Albania, China, and Cambodia (1975-78)—became disaffiliated from the central Soviet revolution. Six others (Congo, Benin, Guinea-Bissau, Cape Verde, Madagascar, and Mozambique) either never became strongly affiliated with the USSR to begin with or gradually drifted away from it. Only seven affiliate revolutions (North Vietnam/Vietnam, Cuba, South Yemen, Ethiopia, Angola, Afghanistan, and Nicaragua) remained affiliated with the USSR from the time they came to power through the collapse of the Marxist-Leninist revolutionary wave (one other affiliate revolution—Grenada—was removed from the wave by the American-led military intervention in 1983). Of course, the subordinate Marxist-Leninist revolutions generally remained subordinate either to the USSR (with Romania and North Korea being partial exceptions) or to Vietnam.

There were six affiliate revolutions within the Arab nationalist revolutionary wave. Two of these (Syria and Iraq) became disaffiliated from the central Egyptian revolution. Three others (Algeria, Sudan, and Libya) never affiliated strongly with it (the Sudanese and Libyan Revolutions occurred after Egypt had abandoned the role of central revolution). Only North Yemen remained affiliated with Egypt from the inception of the North Yemeni Revolution (1962) until Egypt abandoned the role of central revolution following the Arab defeat in the June 1967 Arab-Israeli War.

There have so far been two affiliate revolutions within the Islamic fundamentalist revolutionary wave that remained in power for at least a year.[3] Only one—Sudan—has closely affiliated with Iran.

Far from being a rare event, disaffiliation or lack of strong affiliation with the central revolution has been a frequent occurrence within revolutionary waves. Ten of the eighteen affiliate Marxist-Leninist revolutions (55 percent) fell within these categories, as did five of the six affiliate Arab nationalist revolutions (83 percent) and one of the two affiliate Islamic fundamentalist revolutions (50 percent). Of course, the proportion of disaffiliated and weakly affiliated revolutions within the Islamic fundamentalist revolutionary wave could easily change since, unlike the other two waves, this one has not collapsed.

What accounts for disaffiliation or lack of strong affiliation within a revolutionary wave? One common feature of many, but not all, of the cases in which this occurred is geographic proximity. Although Yugoslavia did not border directly on the USSR, it did border on Marxist-Leninist regimes subordinate to the USSR (Hungary, Romania, and Bulgaria) when it disaffiliated from Moscow in 1948. Similarly, Albania disaffiliated with its neighbor, Yugoslavia, in 1948. When Albania later disaffiliated with the USSR in 1960, it was because the Albanian leadership feared the (unfounded) prospect of a Soviet alliance with its neighbor, Yugoslavia. China disaffiliated with its neighbor, the USSR, in the late 1950s, and armed clashes would later occur along their common frontier. The Khmer Rouge regime that came to power in Cambodia in 1975 disaffiliated primarily with its neighbor, Vietnam, and thus also with the USSR, with which Hanoi was closely allied. Similarly, in the mid-1970s, Vietnam disaffiliated with its neighbor, China. Subordinate Marxist-Leninist regimes, by contrast, neighboring either the USSR or Vietnam, retained this status because they were occupied by Soviet or Vietnamese armed forces that could end any attempt to disaffiliate or withdraw from the revolutionary wave, as they did in East Germany (1953), Hungary (1956), and Czechoslovakia

(1968). Significantly, the two subordinate revolutions in states neighboring the USSR that succeeded in gaining a degree of independence vis-à-vis Moscow were no longer occupied by Soviet troops (Romania and North Korea).

Arab nationalist revolutions did not occur in any of Egypt's immediate neighbors until 1969 (in Sudan and Libya), which was after Cairo had abandoned the role of the central revolutionary state. Neither of its neighbors became closely affiliated with Egypt in the sense of acknowledging Egypt as a leader they would follow. Libya, of course, attempted to take up the role of central revolution, but none of the neighboring states with which it sought to unite (Egypt, Sudan, and Tunisia) strongly affiliated with it in this role. Syria and Iraq, which are neighbors, have been strongly disaffiliated with each other for virtually their entire existence as Arab nationalist revolutionary regimes (1958 until the present). Finally, Iranian relations with the two Islamic fundamentalist regimes in neighboring Afghanistan went from weak affiliation (1992-96) to disaffiliation (after the Taliban seized power in 1996).

By contrast, cases in which close affiliate relationships were maintained until the collapse of a revolutionary wave in the Marxist-Leninist and Arab nationalist waves and up to the present in the Islamic fundamentalist wave have virtually all been between nonneighbors. In the Marxist-Leninist wave, such close affiliations occurred between the USSR on the one hand and North Vietnam/Vietnam, Cuba, South Yemen, Ethiopia, Angola, and Nicaragua on the other. It will never be known if Grenada's Marxist-Leninist regime would have remained closely affiliated with the USSR and Cuba until the collapse of the Marxist-Leninist revolutionary wave, but during the period it was in power (1979-83), it did maintain a close affiliation with them. Close affiliation was also maintained between Egypt and North Yemen from the latter's revolution until Egypt's retreat from the role of central revolution. Finally, close affiliation has so far been maintained between Iran and Sudan since the latter experienced an Islamic fundamentalist revolution in 1989.

The one and only longstanding strong affiliate relationship between neighboring revolutionary regimes was the Soviet-Afghan relationship. During the Soviet occupation of Afghanistan (1979-89), however, Afghanistan was subordinate to the USSR. But before this (i.e., between the emergence of the Afghan Marxist-Leninist regime in April 1978 and the Soviet invasion in December 1979), relations between Moscow and Kabul were often poor. Raymond Garthoff has argued that the Brezhnev leadership persuaded itself that Hafizullah Amin, the top Afghan Marxist-Leninist leader from September to December 1979, whose ultraradical policies served to increase internal opposition to the regime, was actually a CIA agent. When the Soviets invaded at the end of December 1979, they did so to prevent Amin from taking Afghanistan out of the Marxist-Leninist revolutionary wave and from militarily allying his country with the United States, although it is highly doubtful that these were in fact Amin's goals (Garthoff 1985, 918-21).

There is nothing unusual, of course, about neighboring countries having tense or even hostile relations with each other. Except among democracies, this is a normal occurrence in international relations. What is noteworthy, however, is that being part of the same nondemocratic revolutionary wave has not enabled states to overcome the animosities usually experienced between neighbors. Indeed, given the universality of such animosities between neighboring affiliated revolutionary states, it would appear that belonging to the same nondemocratic revolutionary wave only serves to worsen relations between neighbors.

On the other hand, while nonneighboring revolutionary states have shown a greater propensity for maintaining their affiliation with each other, they do not necessarily do so. In the Marxist-Leninist revolutionary wave, six revolutionary states that initially affiliated with the USSR but were quite distant from it geographically (Congo, Benin, Guinea-Bissau, Cape Verde, Madagascar, and Mozambique) drifted away politically from Moscow over time. In the Arab nationalist revolutionary wave, two states not bordering Egypt (Syria and Iraq) strongly disaffiliated with it while another one (Algeria) never affiliated closely with Cairo. Clearly, other explanations are necessary for understanding these cases.

One explanation for why nonneighboring affiliate revolutions drift away from the central revolution is that they either do not need help after they come to power, or that the central revolution either cannot or will not provide it. The Marxist-Leninist regimes in the Congo, Benin, Guinea-Bissau, Cape Verde, and Madagascar, as well as the Arab nationalist regime in Algeria, did not face any strong internal or external challenge when they first came to power. They therefore did not desperately require security assistance from a central revolution or from other states (though, of course, they were happy to receive arms and training to a certain extent). In addition, while the Congo, Benin, Guinea-Bissau, Cape Verde, and Madagascar were desperately in need of economic assistance, this simply was not available to them in any great quantity from the USSR. As time passed, they expanded their economic relations with the West and allowed their affiliation with Moscow to attenuate. Far from being poor, Algeria possessed large oil and natural gas reserves and—despite its economic problems—was a far richer country than Egypt, upon which it was in no way dependent.

In Mozambique, the Marxist-Leninist FRELIMO regime did face a strong security challenge from RENAMO, the opposition group that was supported first by the white minority regime in Rhodesia and later by the white minority regime in South Africa. The Mozambican case is unusual because while the regime there was in need of security assistance, the USSR and Cuba were unwilling to provide this to Mozambique at anywhere near the level that they provided it to Angola and Ethiopia. In addition to support from Zimbabwean troops, though, Mozambique received military training and other aid from Western countries, including the United Kingdom and Portugal (Bowen 1990, 220; Finnegan 1992, 35, 269n2).

As with Algeria, Egypt was not a source of economic assistance to Syria and Iraq (like Algeria, Iraq was rich in oil). After the initial unification between Egypt and Syria, when the Syrian Ba'th party's internal opponents were eliminated, Syria no longer needed Egypt for security assistance, while Iraq never had. Yet this lack of dependence on Egypt does not fully explain either Syria's and Iraq's disaffiliation with it or the extreme animus that arose among Egypt, Syria, and Iraq compared to the general lack of it between Egypt and Algeria. This results from yet another cause of disaffiliation: the attempt by an affiliate revolution to seize the role of central revolution away from the state that has hitherto played it.

An affiliate revolutionary regime's decision to rival the central revolution for leadership results from the ambitions of the former's leadership. Mao Tse-tung, the Syrian Ba'th party, and the Iraqi military leadership apparently concluded not only that they could successfully break with the USSR or Egypt, but also that aspiring revolutionaries and other affiliate revolutions within the wave would shift their loyalty away from Moscow or Cairo and toward Beijing, Damascus, or Baghdad, respectively. In no case did a rival revolution come anywhere near to actually taking over leadership of the revolutionary wave. But even when there were leadership changes in the rival revolutionary regime and its bid for leadership of the revolutionary wave diminished or ended, a close affiliation between it and the central revolution was never reestablished. China and Syria were not willing to accept the status of junior partner once again, and Iraq never was.

In a certain sense, the Iraqi case of instant disaffiliation and rivalry with Egypt is more understandable than the Chinese and Syrian ones, which were closely affiliated with a central revolution at first and then became rivals to it. Why would Mao Tse-tung and the Syrian Ba'th party, whose ambitions to seize the leadership of their respective revolutionary waves were longstanding, accept the position of junior partner vis-à-vis a central revolution at all? In the case of China, Mao had little choice but to accept this status once the Korean War began (less than one year after he had been in power) and led to direct Sino-American conflict that in turn made China dependent on the USSR for military support (Ulam 1974, 530-34). It was only after Stalin died, the Korean War and direct Sino-American conflict ended, and China was no longer as militarily dependent on the USSR that Mao launched his bid for leadership of the Marxist-Leninist revolutionary wave.

Malcolm Kerr has offered an explanation as to why the Syrian Ba'th party accepted what proved to be the position of junior partner within the United Arab Republic:

> The Ba'th was an ideological party, and its leaders suffered the common illusion of ideologues everywhere that they possessed a unique vision of the Truth, which was somehow indispensable for effective political action and which could somehow be converted into political power. Nasir had admirable revolutionary instincts, but, as Michel 'Aflaq [one of the leaders of the Syrian Ba'th] indiscreetly told the press just after the inauguration of the union, he was in need of a 'philosophy.' This, implicitly, the Ba'th would provide.... For what revolution could be preserved without a guiding creed? Surely before long Nasir would be brought by his own experience to acknowledge this need, and would turn to the Ba'th (Kerr 1971, 12).

This expectation, of course, was not fulfilled. Michael Hudson has suggested that the willingness of the Yemeni Socialist party to merge the less-populous South Yemen it ruled with more populous North Yemen in 1990 was based on the expectation that the South "could eventually imprint *nidham* [discipline] on their much larger partner, and thus achieve the progress and development that had always been the ideological beliefs of the YSP" (1995, 22). Like the Syrian Ba'th party, the YSP had expectations about the role it would play after merging with a more populous state that proved illusory. But unlike Syria, which was able to secede from the union with geographically discontiguous Egypt in 1961, South Yemen was defeated militarily when it attempted to secede from the union with neighboring North Yemen in 1994.

The three causes of disaffiliation or weak affiliation cited here (animosities between neighbors, no strong need for or inability to obtain sufficient security and/or economic assistance from the central revolution, and attempts to rival the central revolution for leadership of the revolutionary wave) all have a common element: divergent interests. Although ideological affinity may significantly encourage revolutionary regimes to initially affiliate closely with the central revolution, close affiliation does not last (or, in some cases, even take root) if the interests of the affiliate revolution diverge significantly from those of the central revolution.

LASTING AFFILIATION

Under what conditions do the interests of a central revolution and an affiliate revolution converge sufficiently to maintain a long-term alliance? It is important first to note three sets of circumstances that do not necessarily lead to lasting affiliation but that are sometimes mistakenly thought to be associated with it.

First, lasting affiliation with a central revolution does not necessarily occur just because a central revolution assisted aspiring revolutionaries come to power. Despite the major assistance that the USSR provided to the Yugoslav revolutionaries in the final stages of their struggle with the Germans, they disaffiliated with Moscow less than four years after coming to power. Similarly, although the Albanian Marxist-Leninists received major assistance from their Yugoslav comrades, Albania disaffiliated with Yugoslavia in 1948. The Soviet contribution to the success of the Chinese Marxist-Leninists was not insignificant, but China disaffiliated with the USSR in the late 1950s. Despite having received major assistance from Hanoi (and through it, Moscow), the Khmer Rouge immediately disaffiliated with Vietnam and the USSR after coming to power in Cambodia. Although Egypt provided some military assistance to the aspiring revolutionaries in Algeria, they did not strongly affiliate with Egypt after they came to power. Similarly, the Islamic fundamentalist forces that came to power in Afghanistan in 1992 did not closely affiliate with Iran even though they received some support from it before they ousted the Marxist-Leninist regime in Kabul.

On the other hand, lasting affiliations have occurred between central and affiliate revolutionary regimes where the former made no contribution at all to the victory of aspiring revolutionaries in the latter. The USSR played virtually no role in the coming to power of Marxist-Leninist regimes in Cuba, South Yemen, and Ethiopia, yet the revolutionary regimes in these three countries became closely affiliated with Moscow after coming to power and remained so for the duration of the Marxist-Leninist revolutionary wave. Similarly, Iran appears to have played no role in the coming to power of the Sudanese Islamic fundamentalist regime in 1989, yet Khartoum and Tehran have been closely affiliated since then.

This shows that the degree of military support a central (or affiliate or rival) revolutionary regime gives to aspiring revolutionaries in another country is not a good indicator of whether there will be a close, lasting affiliation between those aspiring revolutionaries that succeed and their benefactors. The new revolutionary regime's decision to affiliate or disaffiliate with a central revolution is based on its calculation of its interests once in power. And based on the number of times that the leaders of affiliate revolutionary regimes have disaffiliated with a central revolution even though it had helped them come to power, gratitude for this support does not appear to play a large role in calculating their interests afterward.

Second, the level of economic support provided by a central revolution does not appear to be an important factor in determining whether an affiliate revolution remains affiliated. The three central revolutions in the three revolutionary waves being considered here have been either unwilling or unable to provide much in terms of economic assistance to their respective affiliate revolutionary regimes. Indeed, the USSR often provided more economic assistance to non-Marxist regimes in the Third World than it did to Marxist ones (Bach 1987). While the leaders of affiliate revolutionary regimes want economic assistance, this is usually only of secondary importance to them. Economic assistance and investment have been available mainly from the status quo Western powers. If seeking aid and investment were the primary goal, revolutionary regimes would not affiliate closely or perhaps at all—with a central revolution, not only because little is available from them but also because a revolutionary regime that closely affiliates with a central revolution usually alienates the status quo powers to the point of depriving itself of the aid and investment that might otherwise be available from them. A revolutionary regime does this, then, because it values close affiliation with a central revolution more highly than it does maximizing aid and investment from all potential sources, including the West. This also holds true for those few Marxist-Leninist regimes, such as Cuba, that received major economic assistance from the USSR. For no matter how much Havana received from Moscow, Castro deprived his country of the far greater and more useful aid and investment his country might otherwise have received from the West. On the other hand, the revolutionary regime's decision to prioritize economic growth is usually accompanied by the decision to abandon revolutionary goals— such as the spread of revolution to other countries and close affiliation with a central revolution—since those goals are incompatible with developing friendly relations with, and obtaining aid and investment from, the status quo powers.

Third, ideological affinity does not necessarily lead to lasting affiliation. It might appear that disputes over ideology were at the center of rifts between central and disaffiliated revolutions, such as those between the USSR and Yugoslavia, the USSR and China, and Egypt and Syria. But before these rifts occurred, ideological differences were either not evident or not important. Yugoslavia's Tito was enthusiastically pro-Soviet from the time he came to power until Stalin sought to depose him. Despite Mao's disagreement with Leninist ideology about the type of revolution appropriate for China, he did not disaffiliate with the USSR while Stalin was still alive and while Mao needed his support. Similarly, at the time of the ill-fated 1958 Egyptian-Syrian union, the ideological viewpoints of the Nasirists and the Syrian Ba'th party "appeared indistinguishable" (Kerr 1971, 6). In each case, an ideological critique of the central revolution by the disaffiliating regimes was made later in order to justify their disaffiliation in revolutionary terms.

Revolutionary ideology is often dogmatic. Those who adhere to it are usually intolerant of those who question it. But far from being rigid and unchanging, revolutionary ideology possesses a degree of malleability for the revolutionary leaders who are its high priests. As their interests and policies change, they can modify their revolutionary ideology accordingly. While this involves risks, an ideological shift from regarding another nation's leaders to one's own as the source of revolutionary knowledge and inspiration is usually successful since it conforms to nationalist fears and resentments of foreign influence. Affiliate revolutions do not blindly follow the lead of central revolutions just because the ideology formulated by the latter expects or demands that the former will do so. When the interests of an affiliate revolutionary regime diverge from those of a central revolution, ideological differences often appear suddenly. Similarly, where there are diverging ideologies but converging interests, the ideological differences tend to be played down by both sides.

It is only under one special set of conditions that lasting affiliation between an affiliate (as opposed to a subordinate) revolution on the one hand and a central revolution on the other occurs: when the affiliate seeks military assistance in combatting a serious security threat, and the central revolution (and perhaps other affiliate revolutions) provides significant military assistance. These conditions were present in all cases in which a lasting affiliation was maintained from the emergence of an affiliate revolution to either the collapse of the wave in the Marxist-Leninist and Arab nationalist cases, or to the present in the Islamic fundamentalist one.

After successfully battling the French, North Vietnam became increasingly involved in conflict not only with U.S.-backed South Vietnam, but with the United States itself. Hanoi obtained significant military assistance from both the USSR and China, and was able to take advantage of the competition between them to avoid becoming exclusively affiliated with either. With the American withdrawal from Indochina in 1973 and the triumph of Marxism-Leninism throughout the region in 1975, Hanoi came to face a new security challenge from both China and its Khmer Rouge allies. Unable to play Moscow and Beijing off each other any more, Hanoi in 1978 (the year Vietnam invaded Cambodia) turned to Moscow for military support against Beijing, and Moscow provided greater quantities than it had even at the height of American involvement in Indochina (Pike 1987, 139). Although Vietnam easily fended off a Chinese attack on its northern border in 1979, it was never able to defeat the insurgency against the Hanoi-installed regime in Cambodia, even though it maintained over 150,000 troops there.

In 1975-76, the fledgling Marxist-Leninist MPLA regime in Angola needed Cuban troops and Soviet arms to defeat a strong challenge posed by its rivals, FNLA and UNITA, which were receiving military support from the United States and South Africa. But the MPLA regime would again have to call upon Cuban troops, along with Soviet arms and advisers, to confront a resurgent threat from UNITA (backed first by South Africa and later by the United States as well). Despite their combined efforts, the USSR, Cuba, and the MPLA succeeded only in containing UNITA, not defeating it.

Although anti-American, the Marxist-Leninist regime that came to power in Ethiopia in 1974 did not become firmly allied with the USSR until 1977 when neighboring Somalia launched an attack to seize the Somali-inhabited Ogaden region. Although Somalia was then allied with the USSR and Cuba, both sacrificed their alliance with Mogadishu by responding positively to Addis Ababa's plea for military assistance. Soviet arms and advisers, as well as Cuban troops, played a key role in beating back the Somali challenge in 1978. This did not, however, bring an end to the security threats faced by the Ethiopian Marxist-Leninist regime. The USSR (without Cuba) provided military assistance against the chronic secessionist insurgency in Eritrea (which the Marxist-Leninist regime in Addis Ababa inherited from the imperial regime it ousted) as well as insurgencies that broke out in Tigray and other parts of the country. As with the resurgent UNITA threat to the MPLA, the Eritrean and Tigrayan insurgencies could not be defeated, but only contained.

The security threat faced by the Marxist-Leninist regime in Afghanistan was so great that it could not be defeated even with the assistance of over 100,000 Soviet troops for nearly a decade against the mujahadin, who were receiving military assistance from many nations. Similarly, the Sandinistas in Nicaragua received military assistance from both Cuba and the USSR in fighting the U.S.-backed contras that were attempting to topple them throughout the 1980s.

Fidel Castro's regime in Cuba fended off the U.S.-sponsored Bay of Pigs invasion in 1961 and weathered the U.S. naval blockade during the Cuban Missile Crisis in 1962. It may be argued that Castro never faced another serious threat to his rule after these events, and therefore his lasting affiliation with the USSR cannot be explained on this basis. However, Castro's sense of threat from the United States never seems to have diminished after 1961-62 (Post 1995). The entire history of Soviet-Cuban relations was characterized by constant Cuban efforts to secure an increased defense commitment from Moscow, and Soviet reluctance to risk another crisis with the United States. Although Castro could not get everything he wanted from the USSR, there was no other source of support against what he saw as the undiminished threat from the United States, and so Cuba remained closely affiliated with Moscow (Katz 1983, 105-9; Blasier 1991).

The Marxist-Leninist regime in South Yemen also faced a number of opposition groups backed either by North Yemen or Saudi Arabia from the time it came to power in 1967 until the mid-1970s, but after that they largely disappeared (Katz 1986, 76-78). As with Cuba, however, the sense of an American threat never diminished until the Marxist-Leninist revolutionary wave collapsed. Aden's fears were not completely unfounded: Bob Woodward has revealed that the CIA did send sabotage teams into South Yemen, but one of these was captured in 1982 and the operation was halted (1987, 215). Although hardly equivalent to the Bay of Pigs operation or the Cuban Missile Crisis, the incident heightened the regime's conviction that the United States sought its overthrow.

North Yemen was the one regime in the Arab nationalist revolutionary wave to maintain a lasting affiliation with Egypt. Although it ousted the monarchy in September 1962, the new Yemen Arab Republic did not capture the monarch who fled the capital and rallied support from the northern tribes. A fierce civil war ensued, in which, for the next five years, as many as 60,000 Egyptian troops along with Yemeni republican forces were unable to defeat the Saudi-backed Yemeni royalists.

Sudan, the one Islamic fundamentalist regime to maintain a lasting affiliation with Iran, has fought secessionist movements in the non-Muslim southern part of the country since coming to power in 1989. Iran has provided military assistance throughout, but even with it, Khartoum has been unable to defeat the non-Muslim secessionists. It should be noted, though, that Iran's contribution to containing Sudan's security threat has not been great compared to those of the Soviet Union and Egypt to the affiliate revolutions with which they maintained long-lasting alliances (Cordesman 1994, 34-35).

The motivation for affiliate revolutions to maintain a long-lasting alliance with a central revolution in these cases was clear: they badly needed military support. But what motivated central revolutions to provide substantial military assistance over long periods for what often proved to be fruitless causes? There appears to have been several motives. First, the central revolutionary regimes seem to have expected that military victory could be achieved quickly and easily, and they did not anticipate that they would turn into such quagmires as Angola, Ethiopia, Cambodia, Afghanistan, and Nicaragua (for the USSR and its allies) or North Yemen (for Egypt).

Second, central revolutions were optimistic not only that military assistance would lead to the consolidation of an affiliate revolution, but also that the prospects were good for extending the revolutionary wave to neighboring countries. This optimism may have been fed by the enthusiasm of the new affiliate revolutionary regime for exporting revolution with assistance from the central revolution and other affiliates. When it first came to power, the Arab nationalist regime in North Yemen sought to export its brand of revolution to its neighbors and create a "Republic of the Arabian Peninsula" (Halliday 1974, 109). Several affiliate Marxist-Leninist revolutions actively sought to support similar revolutions: Yugoslavia in Greece; China in the Third World generally; North Vietnam in the rest of Indochina; Cuba in Latin America (and later in Africa); South Yemen in North Yemen, Oman, and the Arabian Peninsula as a whole; Angola in Zaire, Namibia, and South Africa; and Nicaragua in the rest of Central America. Iran and

Sudan both seek the spread of Islamic revolution throughout the Middle East and Africa. The export of revolution, however, can serve to harm relations between a central revolution and an affiliate one if the two possess different degrees of commitment to this policy. Such differences contributed to the Soviet rifts with Yugoslavia and China.

Third, the vulnerability of these affiliate revolutions provided central revolutions with a greater opportunity to exercise influence over them than was the case with less vulnerable affiliate revolutions. Egypt's role in the leadership politics of North Yemen was so strong during the years of its military involvement that at one point 'Abd al-Nasir kept the North Yemeni president, al-Sallal, under house arrest in Cairo for almost a year (Kerr 1971, 112). In South Yemen, the USSR played an important role in determining the outcome of the leadership struggle that resulted in civil war there in 1986 (Katz 1988-89; Cigar 1989). The USSR, of course, was directly responsible for installing Babrak Karmal in office when it invaded Afghanistan in 1979 (Garthoff 1985, 912-15). The replacement of Karmal by Najibullah in 1986 appears to have occurred at Moscow's initiative as well (Rubinstein 1992, 211). Similarly, Vietnam was directly responsible for installing Heng Samrin in Cambodia after invading that country in 1978 (Garthoff 1985, 716). The USSR, however, apparently did not play a strong role in the leadership politics of other close affiliate revolutions, such as Cuba, North Vietnam/Vietnam, Ethiopia, and Nicaragua. It is possible, of course, that local fear of the large Soviet and other affiliate military and intelligence presence served to constrain the leaders of these affiliate revolutions from pursuing policies Moscow objected to.

A central revolution's optimism about quickly defeating a new affiliate revolutionary regime's opponents and easily exporting revolution to neighboring countries often proved to be ill-founded. Its enthusiasm for exercising strong influence in a chronically unstable regime may also have waned with time. But even if these motives for providing military assistance disappeared, there was one other motive for continuing such support: the fear that if the central revolution ended or sharply curtailed its assistance, the affiliate regime would be overthrown. This would mean not only the loss of an affiliate revolution, but possibly the birth of a perception among other affiliate revolutionary regimes and the status quo powers that the central revolution was no longer willing or able to defend the revolutionary wave. The central revolution feared encouraging the status quo powers to step up their efforts against its revolutionary wave, and other affiliate revolutions to seek security through making peace with the status quo powers. It is noteworthy that both Egypt on the one hand and the USSR and various combinations of its allies on the other kept up their military involvement in unwinnable causes right up to or even beyond the point at which their respective revolutionary waves had begun to collapse.

THE ISLAMIC FUNDAMENTALIST WAVE:
PROSPECTS FOR DISAFFILIATION

There is no guarantee that the patterns of affiliation and disaffiliation that emerged in the Marxist-Leninist, Arab nationalist, or Islamic fundamentalist revolutionary waves will persist in an expanded Islamic fundamentalist revolutionary wave. Indeed, though at this point there is no guarantee that the Islamic fundamentalist revolutionary wave will expand any further than it has, it seems likely that it will. This section will first discuss the implications for the future of the Islamic fundamentalist revolutionary wave if the patterns of affiliation and disaffiliation evident in previous revolutionary waves continue. I will then examine whether the Islamic fundamentalist revolutionary wave differs sufficiently from the Marxist-Leninist and Arab nationalist ones (as well as its own past) in order for previous patterns of affiliation and disaffiliation to be irrelevant to it in the future.

Previous experience in the Marxist-Leninist and Arab nationalist revolutionary waves shows that neighboring revolutionary regimes almost always either disaffiliate or only loosely affiliate with each other. The two existing neighboring Islamic fundamentalist revolutionary regimes—Iran and Afghanistan—conform to this pattern: they have not strongly affiliated with each other (1992-96), or their relations have been adversarial (since the Taliban came to power in 1996). This implies, of course, that as more Islamic revolutionary regimes come into existence, those neighboring each other are likely to be adversaries.

Previous experience in the Marxist-Leninist and Arab nationalist revolutionary waves shows that disaffiliation or weak affiliation occurs when revolutionary regimes have no strong need for military assistance from one another. There is no way to predict whether emerging Islamic fundamentalist revolutionary regimes will face serious security threats. Some may while others may not. However, if the established pattern continues, then those Islamic fundamentalist revolutionary regimes not facing serious security threats are unlikely to accept being the junior partner for long.

The experience of the Marxist-Leninist and Arab nationalist revolutionary waves further suggests that Iran may well be confronted with one or more rivals for its position as central revolution if the Islamic fundamentalist revolutionary wave expands. Whether, or to what extent, this occurs, of course, is also impossible to predict. Comparing the structure of this revolutionary wave with that of the Marxist-Leninist and Arab nationalist ones, however, may indicate the potential for rivalry in an expanded Islamic fundamentalist one.

An important difference between the Marxist-Leninist and the Arab nationalist revolutionary waves was the degree to which the central revolution was more powerful than the affiliates. The USSR was a superpower unquestionably stronger than the other Marxist-Leninist regimes. China was the only other Marxist-Leninist state that could have rivaled the USSR economically and militarily. And while many Marxist-Leninist revolutions disaffiliated with the USSR, China was indeed the only one to rival it. Egypt under 'Abd al-Nasir, by contrast, was not a superpower, but a strong regional power. Its military strength was greater than that of other Arab states, but not to the same extreme degree. And, in fact, there were several aspirants to the role of central revolution in the Arab nationalist revolutionary wave: Syria, Iraq, and (later) Libya.

The Islamic fundamentalist revolutionary wave more closely resembles the Arab nationalist one in terms of Iran's power compared to other actual or potential affiliate revolutions. Like Egypt, Iran is not a superpower but a strong regional power. It is not overwhelmingly powerful compared to many other states where Islamic fundamentalist revolution has the potential to occur. Since there are several countries (including Egypt, Iraq, Algeria, and others) in which Islamic revolution is possible that have the potential to rival Iran economically and militarily, Iran may be confronted with several rivals for the leadership of the Islamic fundamentalist revolutionary wave just as Egypt was in the Arab nationalist one.

Assuming previous patterns of disaffiliation hold true, then, this analysis would suggest that an expanded Islamic revolutionary wave is highly likely to experience disaffiliation within it. What are the prospects for lasting affiliation in this revolutionary wave? Previous patterns show that this can occur when an affiliate revolution faces a security threat for which it seeks military assistance from the central revolution (sometimes in conjunction with other affiliate revolutions). It is difficult to imagine this not happening in an expanded Islamic fundamentalist revolutionary wave. Indeed, the three existing Islamic fundamentalist regimes in Iran, Sudan, and Afghanistan have all faced security threats to a greater or lesser extent. Nor will the divisions affecting many of the nations where Islamic fundamentalist revolution is possible necessarily be healed if it actually occurs. In many cases, these divisions may actually be exacerbated. Many may face external threats as well. Those that face either, or both, are likely to be highly motivated to seek external military assistance.

But previous patterns of lasting affiliation have shown that an embattled affiliate revolution seeking military assistance is not sufficient cause for this to occur. A central revolution must be willing and able to provide this assistance to a great extent and over a long period of time (a lesser degree of need or of commitment is insufficient to sustain a lasting affiliation). Would Iran be willing and able to do this? The answer depends partly on the specific situation—something that cannot be predicted— but also on Iran's capabilities. Here also, comparing the structure of the Islamic fundamentalist revolutionary wave with that of the Marxist-Leninist and Arab nationalist ones may indicate Iran's potential for playing this role.

A central revolution's power compared to affiliate revolutions is highly important in determining its capacity for providing substantial military assistance to embattled affiliates over an extended period of time. Because of its enormous strength measured both in absolute terms and in comparison with affiliate Marxist-Leninist revolutions, the USSR was able to sustain costly military assistance to several affiliate Marxist-Leninist revolutions facing serious security threats, for decades in some cases. Egypt, by contrast, was only able to sustain costly military assistance to one affiliate Arab nationalist regime (North Yemen) facing a serious security threat. However, it did so for just five years, and even then only with significant assistance from the USSR.

Since, like Egypt and unlike the USSR, Iran is not overwhelmingly powerful vis-à-vis other actual or potential affiliate revolutionary regimes, there is reason to doubt whether Iran is capable of making a protracted military commitment to defending one or more embattled affiliates. Egypt and Iran, of course, are not exactly alike. Egypt was a poor country when it played the role of central revolution while Iran is rich in oil. Iran, then, can afford to buy weapons that Egypt could not. Egypt, though, was able to obtain enormous quantities of weapons from the USSR without paying for them (Whelan and Dixon 1986, 186). By contrast, the Islamic Republic of Iran has generally had to purchase its arms imports with hard currency (Cordesman 1994, 38-42). Despite its far greater wealth, Iran under the ayatollahs has been in a less advantageous position to obtain weapons from abroad than was Egypt under 'Abd al-Nasir.

Despite this, Iran, of course, has the means to provide military assistance to an embattled affiliate if it so chooses. Does it have the will? This too cannot be answered precisely; Iran may be more willing to defend an embattled affiliate revolution in some cases than in others. But this is not wholly a hypothetical question; Iran already has a track record vis-à-vis embattled affiliates. It did virtually nothing to prevent the Islamic/democratic regime in Tajikistan that came to power in early 1992 from being overthrown completely by the end of that same year. Nor has Iran done much to assist the increasingly radicalized Islamic opposition to the Soviet-style apparatchik regime that was restored and kept in place with the help of Russian and Uzbek armed forces. While not uncritical of Moscow's use of force here, Tehran has, at Russia's urging, attempted to mediate between the Tajik government and the opposition. Iran seemed to go beyond "evenhandedness" in this dispute when in July 1995 Iranian President Rafsanjani welcomed Tajik President Rakhmonov to bilateral talks in Tehran. At that time, Iran agreed to provide a 10 million dollar loan to Tajikistan. These events are worrisome to the Tajik opposition since they appear to signal "that Iran is drifting towards support for the neo-communist Tajik government."[4]

Iran has provided military assistance to the Islamic fundamentalist regime in Sudan, which has been fighting against non-Muslim secessionist movements in the southern part of the country. But Iran's commitment to Sudan appears to be much smaller than the USSR's to several of its embattled Third World Marxist-Leninist allies or Egypt's to North Yemen. Iranian forces are not fighting in Sudan as Soviet forces did in Afghanistan, Cuban forces did in Angola and Ethiopia, Vietnamese forces did in Cambodia, or Egyptian forces did in North Yemen. Estimates of the level of weapons supplied by Iran to Sudan vary, but they do not appear to be anywhere near the level that the USSR supplied to its embattled Third World affiliates. Indeed, much of the weaponry Iran supplies to Sudan does not go to fight the southern secessionists, but is shipped to aspiring Islamic fundamentalist revolutionaries in other Arab countries. Iran's commitment to Sudan's defense, then, has so far not been particularly strong (Cordesman 1994, 34-35).

Previous patterns of affiliation within revolutionary waves would indicate that if Sudan is not strongly dependent on Iran for military support, then its affiliation with Iran is not particularly strong either. And indeed, there is some evidence that Sudan is not completely affiliated with Iran even now. In describing Sudanese-Iranian relations, Dr. Hasan Turabi expressed his view that "Sudan does not have much to learn from Iran." According to Turabi, "'there are thousands of Sudanese who know Islam better than the more learned ulama in Iran. . . . The Egyptians and the Saudis are alarmed, but in fact the relationship with Iran doesn't amount to a great deal'" (Turabi 1992, 56). While undoubtedly downplaying Sudan's ties with Iran here, Turabi clearly is not in awe of the Iranian leadership and does not feel duty-bound to accept its guidance. Rather, he is confident that his own country's revolution is equal or even superior to Iran's, and that while the Islamic fundamentalist regime in Sudan may receive some degree of assistance from Iran, Khartoum is not—and does not intend to become—subordinate to Tehran.

It would appear, then, that if previous patterns of affiliation and disaffiliation continue in an expanded Islamic revolutionary wave, there will be no lack of opportunity for disaffiliation in it. Further, given Iran's resemblance to Egypt in the sense of only being a strong regional power which is not that much stronger than other actual or potential affiliate revolutions, an expanded Islamic revolutionary wave may have great potential for internal rivalry. In addition, given the limitations on Iran's ability to sustain military intervention abroad in defense of an embattled affiliate, there is strong doubt as to whether lasting affiliation with Iran will occur, as this is one of the crucial factors underlying lasting affiliation.

But will previous patterns of affiliation and disaffiliation be applicable to an expanded Islamic fundamentalist revolutionary wave? Not necessarily. Indeed, the fact that there have only been two completed revolutionary waves of this type (nondemocratic "for" waves that expand primarily via affiliate revolutions) raises the question of whether a pattern has been established for the Islamic fundamentalist revolutionary wave, much less nondemocratic revolutionary waves in general. But if previous patterns of affiliation and disaffiliation do not hold—if there is less disaffiliation and more lasting affiliation—then this revolutionary wave must somehow differ from the Marxist-Leninist and Arab nationalist ones in terms of affiliation and disaffiliation. Is there evidence of such basic differences?

In order for the Islamic fundamentalist revolutionary wave to have a lesser degree of disaffiliation than the Marxist-Leninist or Arab nationalist revolutionary waves (or than itself in the past), it would have to be able to eliminate or reduce the sources of disaffiliation that afflicted previous revolutionary waves. In other words, the Islamic fundamentalist revolutionary wave must be able to overcome tensions between neighbors, lack of a strong need for security assistance on the part of affiliate revolutions, and rivalry over leadership of the wave. Could this occur?

It could if Islamic fundamentalist revolutionary ideology was able to unite its adherents more tightly than Marxism-Leninism and Arab nationalism did. There are, however, many serious ideological differences within the Islamic fundamentalist movement. The Sunni-Shi'ite split, of course, predates the rise of modern Islamic fundamentalism and has not been overcome by it. There are also divisions within the Shi'ite fundamentalist movement (such as the rivalry between Ayatollah Khomeini and his followers on the one hand and Ayatollah Khoi of Iraq on the other) and within the Sunni fundamentalist movement (such as the rivalry between the Egyptian and Sudanese branches of the Muslim Brotherhood). Indeed, these last two examples indicate that the Islamic fundamentalist revolutionary wave may be even more prone to ideological disagreement than the Marxist-Leninist and Arab nationalist ones. While aspiring Marxist-Leninist or Arab nationalist revolutionaries rarely expressed strong disagreements with the central revolution or its affiliates before coming to power, aspiring Islamic fundamentalist revolutionaries have done just that.

As I have suggested, ideological unity does not necessarily mean that there are no conflicting interests within a revolutionary wave. On the other hand, the expression of ideological differences can indicate the presence of conflicting interests. The fact that ideological differences are common within this revolutionary wave indicates that Islamic fundamentalists in different countries are not pursuing common pan-Islamic interests and goals, but rather what Olivier Roy has termed their separate "Islamo-nationalisms" (1994, 26). The very serious differences between Iran and the aspiring Shi'ite revolutionaries in Iraq indicate that Islamic fundamentalism has not overcome the antagonisms between neighbors that other revolutionary waves experienced (Sachedina 1991, 444; Arjomand 1991, 63-66). The fact that some aspiring Islamic fundamentalist revolutionaries have expressed ideological differences with established Islamic regimes—as the Egyptian Muslim Brotherhood has done vis-à-vis both Iran and Sudan—is indicative not just of a potential for disaffiliation, but for rivalry if the aspiring revolutionaries come to power in Egypt (Auda 1991). Indeed, the combination of the Egyptian Muslim Brotherhood's criticism of Iran alongside its active support for aspiring Sunni revolutionaries in other Arab countries indicates that it is rivaling Iran even before it has come to power.

The Islamic fundamentalist revolutionary wave, then, does not seem immune from the causes of disaffiliation that afflicted the Marxist-Leninist and Arab nationalist revolutionary waves. This being the case, it would appear that previous patterns of affiliation and disaffiliation established in the Marxist-Leninist and Arab nationalist revolutionary waves—and all the problems associated with these patterns—are likely to apply to the Islamic fundamentalist revolutionary wave as well.

Chapter 4

The Collapse of Revolutionary Waves

After the Arab defeat in the June 1967 Arab-Israeli War, the Arab nationalist revolutionary wave experienced a crisis of confidence from which it never recovered. Although Arab nationalist revolutions took place in Sudan and Libya approximately two years after this cathartic event, none has taken place since then. The Arab nationalist regime in Sudan was ousted in 1985 and ultimately replaced by an Islamic fundamentalist one. The other Arab nationalist regimes are still in power, but instead of serving as revolutionary examples that inspire others, most face a serious threat from Islamic fundamentalist revolutionaries seeking to overthrow them.

The collapse of the Marxist-Leninist revolutionary wave has been even more dramatic. Once it was clear that Soviet leader Mikhail Gorbachev would not use force to defend them, all the subordinate Marxist-Leninist regimes in Eastern Europe were quickly overthrown in the autumn of 1989. The USSR itself disintegrated in 1991. Since then, few avowedly Marxist-Leninist regimes remain in power, and those that do appear to be very much on the defensive. This chapter examines how nondemocratic revolutionary waves that expand via affiliate revolutions collapse.

I will discuss the general conditions present in both the Arab nationalist and Marxist-Leninist revolutionary waves preceding their collapse, the immediate causes of the crises that led their central revolutionary regimes to give up their leadership roles, the fate of the component parts of the two revolutionary waves (particularly the embattled affiliate revolutions that were abandoned by the central revolutions), and the Islamic fundamentalist revolutionary wave's prospects of collapse.

GENERAL PRECEDING CONDITIONS

Certain conditions preceded the collapse of both the Arab nationalist and Marxist-Leninist revolutionary waves: economic failure, military stalemate with states outside the revolutionary wave, rivalry within the wave, and general loss of faith in the revolutionary ideology in the revolutionary states.

It is hardly surprising that both the Arab nationalist and the Marxist-Leninist revolutionary waves experienced economic failure, since both adhered to the same inefficient, unproductive economic model. Indeed, Arab nationalism essentially adopted its economic concepts from Marxism-Leninism. The advocates of this model in both revolutionary waves promised rapid economic growth and improved living standards for the population as a whole. Stalin's apparent success compared to the capitalist West in achieving rapid economic growth and eliminating poverty and unemployment made "scientific socialism" a highly attractive economic model for Arab nationalists and Third World Marxist-Leninists. This model was also attractive because it allowed revolutionary regimes maximum control over their economies by eliminating or severely restricting the role of the domestic private sector and foreign investment.

Although the advocates of scientific socialism lauded Soviet independence from market incentives (which, by their very nature, cannot operate where government controls economic activity), they failed to appreciate that by the late 1950s Soviet economic growth rates had fallen considerably from the forced pace achieved under Stalin, and that the Soviet economy was entering a period of decline from which it would not recover while the USSR clung to scientific socialism. Arab nationalist and Third World Marxist-Leninist leaders saw the Soviet economy as a model to emulate, but for the most part, they succeeded only in replicating or even exceeding its economic failures. Domestic and foreign investment dried up, and unproductive state enterprises were created. Despite the failure of this economic model, leaders in both revolutionary waves continued to pursue it doggedly. As Forrest Colburn explained, "Revolutionary hubris not only shaped many policies, but also leaders' expectations of their potential, which prompted a refusal to retrench when early expectations were confounded" (1994, 61).

It is ironic that economic failure characterized states belonging to a revolutionary wave before it collapsed since it also characterized these states before their revolutions. Goodwin and Skocpol, however, have argued that widespread poverty is not sufficient to spark revolution. While revolution has occurred in many countries experiencing widespread poverty, it has not occurred in all of them (1989, 490). Similarly, although common to virtually all Arab nationalist and Marxist-Leninist regimes, economic failure did not by itself cause the collapse of either of these revolutionary waves. Revolutionary regimes have survived for many years or even decades under deteriorating economic conditions. However, this factor did exacerbate the crises these two revolutionary waves experienced, which led to their collapse.

Both revolutionary waves as a whole were also in a state of military stalemate vis-à-vis outside powers before these crises occurred. Although possessing larger populations and military forces than Israel, the Arab nationalist states by the mid-1960s had not made any progress in destroying the Jewish state and thereby liberating Palestine. By the early 1970s the USSR had achieved nuclear parity with the United States, and the Warsaw Pact states had maintained larger conventional forces than the NATO alliance all along, but Moscow was hard-pressed to keep up with Western technological innovations that strengthened their numerically smaller armed forces. Nor did Moscow successfully promote revolution in or end the American alliances with Western Europe and Japan—the two regions that, along with the United States itself, were the heartland of capitalism and democracy.

These two military stalemates had several important effects. To begin with, they were a serious drain on the revolutionary waves' resources. Of course, they were also a drain on their opponents', but to a lesser degree. The Russian and Egyptian efforts to maintain large military forces further distorted their unproductive economies. The West was able to maintain sufficient armed forces with a relatively smaller share of gross national product from their more productive economies. The United States and the USSR also provided military assistance to their allies in Israel and the Arab nationalist wave, respectively. Despite its much smaller size and population, Western-assisted Israel proved to be militarily more powerful than the Soviet-assisted Arab nationalist states (though this would not become evident until 1967).

In addition to these stalemates with their principal adversaries, the central revolutionary regimes (as well as some affiliate regimes in the Marxist-Leninist case) were involved in long, protracted struggles to protect weaker affiliate regimes against their internal opponents (which were often supported by various external status quo powers). In the Arab nationalist revolutionary wave, Egypt intervened militarily to protect the North Yemeni "republicans" against the royalists. In the Marxist-Leninist revolutionary wave, Cuban troops fought to protect the MPLA regime against UNITA in Angola, Vietnamese troops fought to protect the Heng Samrin regime they had installed in Cambodia against the Khmer Rouge and two much less powerful non-Marxist opposition groups, and Soviet troops fought to protect the PDPA regime in Afghanistan against the mujahadin. Cuban troops and Soviet advisers also helped Marxist Ethiopia drive out invading forces from Somalia. In addition, the USSR provided military support to Marxist Ethiopia in its struggle against rebels in Eritrea, Tigray, and other parts of the country, while both the USSR and Cuba assisted the Sandinista regime in Nicaragua in fighting its contra opponents.

As I argued in the previous chapter, security threats to these weak revolutionary regimes created lasting affiliations between them and the central revolutions and/or other stronger affiliate revolutions making strenuous efforts to protect them. This external assistance did succeed—as long as it lasted—in preventing these weak affiliate regimes from being overthrown. On the other hand, this external assistance was never strong enough to defeat the opponents of their embattled affiliates. Further, these conflicts became a chronic drain on the already weak economies of all the states of the revolutionary waves involved in them.

But like economic failure, military stalemates with external forces did not cause the collapse of the Arab nationalist and Marxist-Leninist revolutionary waves. Despite their economic problems, the two central revolutions (and their Cuban and Vietnamese allies in the Marxist-Leninist case) were able to sustain their end of these stalemates for many years. Indeed, they were able to sustain military intervention to protect weak allies as long as or longer than France, the United States, and Portugal did without provoking the domestic unrest that these Western states experienced as a result. But again, like economic failure, military stalemates exacerbated the crises these two revolutionary waves experienced, which led to their collapse.

Both revolutionary waves had also experienced bitter internal rivalry by the time they collapsed. Egypt faced a threat to its leadership of the wave from Syria and Iraq while the USSR was similarly challenged by China. The Sino-Soviet rivalry was costly to both states since it led them each to dramatically increase the military forces deployed along their common border. For Moscow, of course, this simply added to the military stalemate that its failed economy had to support.

Egypt did not face a comparable extra burden since its two main rivals were not its neighbors. But the rivalries within both waves led to an intense internal competition for influence. The rivalry within the two revolutionary waves became so intense that it led on occasion to revolutionary regimes cooperating with status quo powers against other revolutionary regimes. The result of Sino-Soviet rivalry was that China, which had been more virulently anti-American than the USSR at the beginning of their quarrel, came to fear Moscow so much that it entered into a de facto alliance with Washington against the Soviet Union in the early 1970s (Garthoff 1985, 199-247). In 1961, Egypt found itself aligned with conservative Jordan, Saudi Arabia, Kuwait, and its hated enemy, Great Britain, against revolutionary Iraq when Baghdad tried for the first time to annex Kuwait (Kerr 1971, 18-21). Kerr also wrote that while there were many disputes between revolutionary and conservative Arab regimes in the early 1960s, "of all the disputes the most bitter and least soluble was between the rival revolutionary movements of Damascus and Cairo" (1971, 96).

Rivalry within these revolutionary waves did not cause their collapse either. Indeed, in the Marxist-Leninist case, China had long ceased its effort to rival the USSR for leadership of the revolutionary wave by the time the Soviet Union collapsed. Nevertheless, I will argue in the next section that these rivalries contributed to actions on the part of the central revolution that would either lead directly to the crisis associated with collapse (in the Arab nationalist case) or add to the military and economic burdens confronting the central revolution when this crisis arrived (in the Marxist-Leninist one).

Both revolutionary waves experienced a general loss of popular faith in their internationalist revolutionary ideologies—especially in the central revolutionary states. Certainly by the time Brezhnev was in power, popular enthusiasm for Marxism-Leninism in the Soviet Union had all but disappeared. Marxism-Leninism was even less popular in the subordinate revolutionary regimes of Eastern Europe, where the USSR had to use force to maintain it in three instances (East Germany, 1953; Hungary, 1956; and Czechoslovakia, 1968) and threatened to do so in two others (Poland, 1956 and 1981). The genuine enthusiasm of the Egyptian public for 'Abd al-Nasir had waned between the 1950s and mid-1960s, even before the debacle of June 1967. The succession of self-proclaimed Arab nationalist regimes in Syria and Iraq also enjoyed little popular support.

Several factors have been cited as causes of the loss of revolutionary faith, including the regimes' economic failure, foreign policy failure, repressiveness, and general inability to achieve their promised goals. It must be noted, though, that this loss of faith was not nearly as great in the Arab nationalist revolutionary wave before its great crisis (the June 1967 War) as it was in the USSR and Eastern Europe long before the collapse of the Marxist-Leninist revolutionary wave. The Arab defeat in 1967, though, caused a profound loss of faith in Arab nationalism (Ajami 1992).

But the loss of popular faith in the central revolutionary states was also insufficient to cause the collapse of their respective revolutionary waves. The regime in Moscow faced no serious domestic challenge for decades before the collapse of the Marxist-Leninist revolutionary wave, notwithstanding the lack of popular support for its rule or its ideology. Despite the existence of opposition movements inside Egypt, these did not pose a serious challenge to 'Abd al-Nasir's regime.

Indeed, before the collapse of these two revolutionary waves, the loss of faith in the central revolutionary states seemed to have no impact on aspiring revolutionaries elsewhere. Long after Marxism-Leninism lost whatever inspirational force it had in the USSR, it inspired successful revolutions in several Third World nations, especially during the 1970s. Similarly, despite increasing awareness in Egypt of the harsh reality of 'Abd al-Nasir's rule, every successful revolution in the Arab world from 1952 through 1969 (except the Marxist-Leninist one in South Yemen) was Arab nationalist. The principal opposition movements to the conservative Arab monarchies that did not succumb to revolution were also Arab nationalist during this period, and even for some time after it.

Crane Brinton noted this contradiction in the Marxist-Leninist revolutionary wave between the strength of a revolutionary ideology in countries where it had not yet occurred and its weaknesses in those where it already had when he wrote that, "The Marxist heaven on earth will do as a mere promise" in Third World countries where Marxist-Leninist revolution had not come to power "for a while; but in Moscow, it has got pretty soon to become in part visible—or the whole doctrine must undergo a still unpredictable transformation" (1965, 233). Albert Hourani made a similar observation about the Arab nationalist revolutionary wave when he noted that the strength of its revolutionary ideology declined after coming to power: "Once political ideas were appropriated by governments, they were in danger of losing their meaning. They became slogans which grew stale by repetition, and could no longer gather other ideas around them into a powerful constellation, mobilize social forces for action, or turn power into legitimate authority" (1991, 454).

Central revolutions, then, were able to withstand the popular loss of faith in the revolutionary ideology as well as take advantage of popular enthusiasm for it in other countries for a significant period of time. But this loss of faith in the central revolutions would also play an important role in exacerbating the crises these two revolutionary waves experienced, while enthusiasm for the ideology among affiliate revolutions and aspiring revolutionaries (to the extent it survived) would not be enough to prevent the waves from collapsing.

ABANDONING THE ROLE OF CENTRAL REVOLUTION

Both the Arab nationalist and the Marxist-Leninist revolutionary waves experienced severe crises of confidence that led Egypt and Russia to abandon the role of central revolution. The crises had two factors in common: 1) overoptimism about the weakness of status quo opponents, as well as competition with rival revolutionary regimes, which led the central revolution to become involved in military ventures that were unsuccessful and that added significantly to its burdens; and 2) the top leadership's loss of confidence not only in its ability to lead the revolutionary wave, but about the desirability of doing so. In both cases, this crisis led to a decision by the leadership of the central revolution to abandon its military support for its embattled affiliate revolutions in return for cooperation and assistance from its once reviled status quo opponents. I will describe the crisis of confidence in the Arab nationalist revolutionary wave first since it occurred first.

The Arab Nationalist Crisis of Confidence

'Abd al-Nasir became widely acknowledged throughout the Arab world as leader of the Arab nationalist revolutionary wave, not so much because he led the first successful Arab nationalist revolution, but because of his foreign policy successes after he came to power. After being refused arms by the West, Cairo signed an arms agreement with Czechoslovakia (actually the USSR) in September 1955—the first major Soviet bloc weapons accord with a Third World country. In July of the following year, after the United States withdrew its offer to aid in the construction of the Aswan High Dam, 'Abd al-Nasir announced the nationalization of the Suez Canal, which was still being run by Britain and France even after Egypt had become independent (Lenczowski 1980, 528-31). While these two actions alone increased 'Abd al-Nasir's prestige as a leader who "stood up to" the West, this image was burnished to an extraordinary degree by the Suez

War. In October 1956, a coordinated action was launched in which Israel invaded the Sinai Peninsula and Britain and France intervened to "protect" the Suez Canal. Largely under American pressure, though, Britain and France halted their invasion and withdrew from the Canal, and a few months later Israel gave up the territory it had captured. Although his forces had not been able to defend Egypt's positions and it was actually American actions that had saved him, 'Abd al-Nasir successfully claimed the credit within the Arab world for having "defeated" the British, French, and Israeli forces. George Lenczowski observed, "Thus, rather paradoxically, out of the military defeat in Sinai there grew around Egypt's regime and its leader an aura of victory and invincibility which greatly enhanced their prestige in the Arab world" (1980, 536).

One of the dividends of this greatly enhanced prestige was the decision by the Syrian Ba'th party to merge Syria with Egypt into the United Arab Republic under 'Abd al-Nasir's leadership in February 1958. 'Abd al-Nasir hoped and expected that other Arab countries would also join the UAR, but none did. Further, the Syrian military ousted the Egyptian administration and reasserted Syria's independence in September 1961, dealing a severe blow to both 'Abd al-Nasir's ambitions and his prestige. Malcolm Kerr wrote that in addition to increasing repression at home, Cairo responded to this setback by reversing the moderate policy it had been following toward other Arab states since 1959 and "assumed the stance of the militant revolutionary, uncompromisingly dedicated to the overthrow of all its conservative neighbors" (1971, 25).

Its first opportunity came in North Yemen the following September when a Nasirist coup (which Egypt appears to have helped organize) toppled the monarchy and declared the Yemen Arab Republic. Had all gone well, the royalist opposition would have been quickly defeated and North Yemen could have served as a base to spread Arab nationalist revolution to British-ruled South Yemen, and more importantly, oil-rich Saudi Arabia. The fact that there was a power struggle going on within the Saudi royal family between the incompetent King Sa'ud and Crown Prince Faysal (who would finally depose his elder brother in 1964), and that one of the princes (Talal bin 'Abd al-'Aziz) and several Saudi air force officers defected from the Kingdom to Egypt shortly after the North Yemeni Revolution, gave rise to speculation that Saudi Arabia was also ripe for Arab nationalist revolution (Halliday 1974, 55–56, 67; Holden and Johns 1981, 198–240). The rapid dispatch of Egyptian troops to North Yemen may also have been seen by Cairo as insurance that the revolutionary regime there would not be in a position to renounce its affiliation with Egypt, as Syria had done, or to affiliate with 'Abd al Nasir's Syrian or Iraqi rivals.

But 'Abd al-Nasir's assumptions about North Yemen proved to be overoptimistic. He underestimated the ousted Yemeni king's ability to rally substantial support, as well as the ability and determination of Faysal of Saudi Arabia to back the Yemeni royalist cause. Instead of quickly defeating the Yemen Arab Republic's internal opponents and spreading revolution to Saudi Arabia, 'Abd al-Nasir's forces ended up involved in a protracted effort just to prevent the Yemen Arab Republic's collapse. Far from becoming the asset he had anticipated it would be, North Yemen became a serious liability for 'Abd al-Nasir despite the fact that it remained loyally affiliated with Egypt.

By mid-1967, 'Abd al-Nasir's forces were still bogged down in North Yemen, and Egyptian rivalry with both conservative and revolutionary Arab regimes had intensified. According to Kerr, Egypt, Syria, and Jordan (the three states Israel would defeat) did not seek war with Israel. The hostile gestures they made were not so much directed at it as at one another. Egypt's bellicosity was intended to prevent Syria from claiming that 'Abd al-Nasir was not strongly committed to the cause of liberating Palestine, and from winning leadership of the Arab nationalist revolutionary wave. Syria's aggressiveness was meant to undercut Egypt and the Jordanian monarchy. Jordan sought to secure Egyptian protection against Syria. The Israelis, however, saw their neighbors' hostility as threatening and preempted what they thought was an imminent Arab attack by attacking first. In less than a week, the numerically smaller Israeli armed forces had captured the Gaza Strip and Sinai Peninsula from Egypt, the West Bank from Jordan, and the Golan Heights from Syria (Safran 1969, 317-82).

The devastating Arab defeat in 1967 initiated a crisis of confidence in the ability of Arab nationalism to realize its grandiose revolutionary goals. 'Abd al-Nasir himself experienced this crisis intensely (Farid 1994). Up to the 1967 War, 'Abd al-Nasir not only failed to achieve his broader Arab nationalist goals, but his pursuit of them had resulted in enormous economic and military burdens that made further pursuit extremely difficult. After the war, 'Abd al-Nasir abandoned his Arab nationalist ambitions in favor of the more limited aim of pursuing Egypt's own interests, including its economic well-being. The focus on this long-neglected objective, Adeed Dawisha pointed out, meant that Egypt "very quickly became dependent on the financial assistance of the oil rich but conservative and pro-Western Arab states, the very states against which 'Abd al-Nasir's radical policies were directed" (1986, 25).

This desperately needed economic assistance from Saudi Arabia, however, came at a price: the withdrawal of Egyptian armed forces from North Yemen. Since this was a burden 'Abd al-Nasir no longer wanted to carry, he readily agreed to this condition and implemented the withdrawal so rapidly that the last Egyptian troops left North Yemen in November 1967 (Kerr 1971, 130). This was not a case of an affiliate revolution disaffiliating with a central revolution, but of a loyal affiliate revolution being abandoned by a central revolution that was in the process of ending its leadership role within the revolutionary wave.

The Marxist-Leninist Crisis of Confidence

The crisis of confidence took longer to develop in the Marxist-Leninist revolutionary wave. It originated in the early 1970s, when the American crisis of confidence, caused by its unsuccessful military intervention in Indochina, was reaching the crescendo that would lead to the complete American withdrawal in early 1973, as well as the "Vietnam syndrome," which made it politically impossible for the U.S. government to undertake large-scale military intervention anywhere in the Third World until the 1991 Gulf War. Along with many in the West, the Soviet leadership in the early 1970s concluded that the United States was on the decline as a world power while the USSR was on the ascent. The Soviet achievement of nuclear parity with the United States, the upsurge of aspiring Marxist-Leninist revolutionaries in many parts of the Third World, and the American unwillingness to become militarily involved there presented opportunities for the expansion of the Marxist-Leninist revolutionary wave. Chinese efforts to establish close contact with some of these aspiring revolutionaries and new revolutionary regimes seemed to goad the Soviet Union into providing greater assistance to them as insurance that they would affiliate with Moscow and not with Beijing.

The 1970s were also the decade of detente between the United States and the USSR. The U.S. government often warned that progress on arms control and Soviet-American relations in general were linked to Soviet behavior in the Third World, but the Soviet leadership had reason to believe otherwise: a pattern emerged in which Soviet-assisted intervention in the Third World by one of Moscow's close affiliates was vociferously decried by Washington with dire warnings about the fate of detente—claims that proved hollow not long after the intervention succeeded (or, in retrospect, appeared to have succeeded). While arms control and detente were valued highly by the Soviet leadership, it seemed to conclude that support for intervention in the Third World would not derail them because, in Moscow's view, the United States, as a declining power, needed detente far more than the USSR did.

It was the Cuban-Soviet intervention in Angola in 1975-76 that set the pattern for what Moscow foresaw as the interaction between detente and active efforts to expand the Marxist-Leninist revolutionary wave in the Third World. As the Portuguese prepared to withdraw from Angola, a three-sided power struggle emerged among the MPLA, UNITA, and FNLA. Moscow and Havana had close ties with the MPLA, China was linked with UNITA, and the United States began to support FNLA and, to a lesser extent, UNITA. The exact sequence of events was quite complicated and will not be described here. Suffice it to say that Cuba sent arms and soldiers to help the MPLA while South Africa did the same to help FNLA and UNITA. Embarrassed by its link with the same group South Africa supported, China ended its involvement altogether. The Ford administration began a covert assistance program to aid the FNLA in particular, but this was ended by Congress in December 1975. After it was clear that the limited U.S. role in the conflict was ending, the USSR became heavily involved in facilitating Cuba's military intervention. The MPLA's enemies were soon defeated. The USSR and its allies appeared not only to have gained a victory in Angola, but to have positioned themselves to assist aspiring Marxist-Leninist revolutionaries in neighboring Namibia and nearby South Africa (Porter 1984, 147-81). And detente also continued, despite Washington's warnings about Soviet behavior in the Third World being linked to arms control.

A similar pattern of events occurred in the Horn of Africa in 1977-78. In 1977, Somalia (which had been allied with the USSR and Cuba since 1969) invaded the Ogaden region of Marxist Ethiopia that Somali nationalists had long regarded as rightfully belonging to them. Although Moscow and Havana hoped at first to mediate this dispute between their two allies, they began sending military assistance to Ethiopia after it was invaded. Mogadishu responded by expelling the Soviet and Cuban presence from Somalia. Moscow and Havana responded in turn by increasing their military aid to Addis Ababa dramatically. With the help of 12,000-15,000 Cuban troops and 1,500 Soviet military advisers, the Somalis were driven out of Ogaden. China was not involved in this conflict. When Mogadishu turned to Washington for help, the Carter administration indicated that it would not help Somalia keep territory it had tried to forcibly wrest from Ethiopia, but would support Somalia if its opponents' forces crossed the border—which they did not. When the fighting was over, the USSR had lost Somalia as an ally to the United States, but had gained a far more important ally in Ethiopia. Furthermore, Soviet-Cuban intervention had once more been victorious (Porter 1984, 182-215). And while Washington again bitterly complained that Soviet and Cuban actions had negative implications for detente, progress on arms control continued.

This pattern of events was repeated in Indochina. Tension between the Marxist-Leninist regimes in Vietnam and Cambodia grew to such an extent that Vietnam invaded Cambodia in December 1978, ousted the pro-Chinese Khmer Rouge regime, and installed a Marxist-Leninist regime subordinate to Hanoi. Vietnamese forces undertook the bulk of the fighting, but the USSR was involved through its supply of arms and transport to Hanoi. The Chinese attempted to "teach Vietnam a lesson" the following February by launching an attack across the Sino-Vietnamese border, but failed either to gain much territory or to force Vietnam to withdraw or even redeploy its forces from Cambodia to its border with China. Although the USSR was not directly involved in this Sino-Vietnamese clash, the signing of a Soviet-Vietnamese Treaty of Friendship and Cooperation the previous year may well have deterred China from pressing its attack more vigorously. The United States condemned the Vietnamese invasion of Cambodia and the Soviet role in assisting it, and gave tacit encouragement to China, but did not become involved in the conflict (Garthoff 1985, 718-26; Rodman 1994, 189-96). Once again, warnings emanated from Washington about the potential negative consequences of the Cambodian invasion on detente, but progress on the SALT II Treaty continued.

Moscow apparently calculated that a negative American reaction to the Soviet invasion of Afghanistan would be as short-lived as it had been in Angola, the Horn of Africa, and Cambodia. An additional factor in its assessment may have been that Washington had accepted the fact that a Marxist-Leninist regime had come to power in Afghanistan in April 1978 and even had diplomatic relations with it. But the Brezhnev leadership badly miscalculated on Afghanistan. Not only did they fail to anticipate that Soviet intervention there would lead to the end of detente and progress on arms control, but they also underestimated the Afghan opposition forces' ability to mount a protracted insurgency against the Marxist-Leninist regime and its Soviet protectors (Ulam 1983, 258-59; Rodman 1994, 207-21).

Afghanistan, though, was not the only country in which affiliate Marxist-Leninist regimes were fighting against externally backed internal opponents. Such insurgencies were also taking place in Angola, Ethiopia, Mozambique, Cambodia, and Nicaragua. Not only were the affiliate Marxist-Leninist regimes in these countries unable to defeat their opponents, but in some cases they were unable to do so even with large numbers of Cuban, Vietnamese, or Soviet troops. Despite the fact that these counterinsurgency efforts were dragging on, the Brezhnev, Andropov, and Chernenko regimes saw the opposition as temporary, likening them to the "Basmachi" (those who opposed the imposition of Soviet rule in Central Asia in the 1920s), who were eventually defeated (Katz 1987, 54-57).

The aged Soviet leadership was unhappy about the end of detente and progress on arms control with the United States, but also seemed to think that this was a temporary problem. The Soviet image of American politics was one in which the American public "demanded" detente with the USSR and an end to U.S. military intervention in the Third World. President Jimmy Carter's withdrawal of the SALT II Treaty from Senate consideration for ratification appeared irrational to Moscow. What was the point of halting progress on arms control, which benefitted the United States as well as the USSR, for the sake of a small country bordering the USSR in which Soviet forces had intervened to protect a Marxist-Leninist regime that Washington had already recognized? During the 1980 American presidential election, Moscow seemed to hope that Ronald Reagan would win since, despite their anti-Soviet rhetoric, the Republicans under Nixon and Ford had established a track record of working with the USSR on detente and arms control. When Reagan's policies in office proved to be as anti-Soviet as his campaign rhetoric, the Soviet leaders seemed to think that he would become as unpopular with the American public as he was with them (Ulam 1983, 287-88; Mills 1990, 176).

Mikhail Gorbachev became general secretary of the Communist party of the Soviet Union in March 1985, approximately four months after Reagan was reelected. Under Gorbachev Moscow began a fundamental reassessment of the USSR's internal and external interests. While his predecessors did not appear to see the Soviet economy as something that needed to be changed significantly, Gorbachev did. He realized that the Soviet economy was stagnating while Western, Chinese, and many capitalist Third World economies were growing rapidly. He understood that if the Soviet economy continued to stagnate, the USSR's military strength vis-à-vis economically strong countries would erode (Aslund 1989, 13-21).

As a result of the overwhelming priority he placed on economic transformation in the USSR, Gorbachev adopted a different view of detente with the United States than his predecessors. While his predecessors thought that it was the United States that needed detente more, Gorbachev understood that a radical transformation of the Soviet economy could not be undertaken without it. In order to obtain the needed resources for economic transformation, the massive Soviet defense budget needed to be cut dramatically. But it would not be possible to do this without detente (White 1990, 155-61).

Further, Gorbachev also developed a different understanding of the relationship between detente with the United States and Soviet behavior in the Third World. While his predecessors thought that cooperation with the United States on issues of mutual concern, such as arms control, could be kept separate from the Soviet-American competition in the Third World, Gorbachev came to understand that large-scale military intervention by the USSR and its allies in the Third World—especially the Soviet invasion of Afghanistan—was the main cause for detente's demise (Sakwa 1990, 346-47; Rubinstein 1992, 199).

Finally, Gorbachev's assessment of the importance of affiliate Marxist-Leninist regimes in the Third World to Moscow was very different than that of his predecessors. During the great wave of Third World Marxist-Leninist revolutions in the 1970s, Moscow saw each additional one as evidence that the Marxist-Leninist revolutionary wave would spread throughout Asia, Africa, and Latin America. Each revolution that occurred seemed to improve the prospects for revolution to spread to still more countries. By the time Gorbachev came to power, however, it was not only doubtful that any more Marxist-Leninist revolutions were going to succeed (the last one to have done so was in Nicaragua in 1979), but the value of these affiliate revolutions to Moscow had clearly diminished. There was an increasing realization that the insurgencies being fought against these regimes were not temporary problems that would soon be satisfactorily resolved, but permanent conditions endemic to these weak, unpopular regimes. Instead of assets, Gorbachev came to see these regimes as liabilities in terms of their permanent instability, the high cost to the USSR of keeping them in power, and the negative effect Soviet involvement in them had on reestablishing detente with the United States, which the new Soviet leader saw as essential for the urgent task of restructuring the USSR's economy.[1]

It took time, however, for Gorbachev to realize the diminished value of affiliate Marxist-Leninist regimes, or the obstacle that Moscow's military involvement in their conflicts posed to the reestablishment of detente and the achievement of his domestic goals. When he first came to power in 1985, Gorbachev responded to the chronic insurgencies plaguing Marxist-Leninist regimes in the Third World not by withdrawing from them but by trying to defeat them once and for all. He helped mount the largest-ever offensives against the opponents of these regimes in all six cases where they occurred, but none succeeded (Katz 1987). By 1987, Gorbachev apparently concluded that these insurgencies could not be ended militarily, and so he attempted to end them diplomatically. Even so, he hoped to secure the survival of these regimes through striking a deal in which Cuban, Vietnamese, and Soviet forces would be withdrawn from Angola, Cambodia, and Afghanistan in exchange for an end to military assistance to insurgent forces in them from the United States and its allies. In the improving climate of detente, just such agreements were reached regarding Afghanistan in April 1988 and Angola in December 1988. Although not part of a formal agreement, Vietnam unilaterally withdrew its troops from Cambodia in September 1989. However, military assistance continued from the USSR and its allies to these embattled regimes, indicating a Soviet desire not to see its loyal affiliates overthrown (Katz 1990a, 353).

Unlike the Arab nationalist revolutionary wave, there was no one single incident like the 1967 Arab-Israeli War that caused the crisis of confidence in the Marxist-Leninist revolutionary wave. While Gorbachev understood that the USSR's economic problems were great and required radical change, he overestimated his ability to make the necessary changes with the existing bureaucracy, which had overseen and benefitted from the old system. His reforms were "too little, too late," and seemed only to lead to an ever deepening economic crisis. Further, instead of providing Gorbachev with greater public support as he seemed to expect, increased freedom of the press and democratization led to greater demands by non-Russians to secede from the USSR. The attempt to repress these demands, which Gorbachev regarded as illegitimate, only served to inflame them (Nahaylo and Swoboda 1990, 231-350).

The point at which Gorbachev definitively signaled the end to Soviet willingness to play the role of the central revolution came during the autumn of 1989 with the collapse of communism in Eastern Europe. Gorbachev understood that efforts to reform the USSR by Khrushchev and, to a lesser extent, Kosygin, had led to crises in Hungary in 1956 and Czechoslovakia in 1968. On both occasions, Soviet troops successfully intervened to prevent the downfall of communism. Also on both occasions, hard-liners who opposed reform in the USSR were able to curtail it by arguing that what had happened in Hungary and Czechoslovakia could happen elsewhere in Eastern Europe or even in the USSR itself. Just as previous Soviet reform efforts had done, Gorbachev's perestroika led to rising discontent in Eastern Europe in the late 1980s. Determined not to allow his conservative opponents the opportunity to crush unrest in Eastern Europe and destroy his own reform efforts, Gorbachev made it clear during the fall of 1989, as the subordinate regimes in Eastern Europe were collapsing, that the USSR would not intervene to protect the increasingly unpopular hard-line East European Communist rulers (Karen Dawisha 1990, 20-21; Gwertzman and Kaufman 1991, 163-65, 271-72).

Despite this enormous loss, Moscow continued some of its efforts to keep the affiliate Third World Marxist-Leninist—which remained loyal to Moscow—in power. Over the next two years, however, Gorbachev became increasingly consumed by his ultimately unsuccessful struggle both to keep himself in office and the USSR together. By the time the USSR collapsed in December 1991, Moscow had abandoned its erstwhile affiliates in the Third World to their various fates. As with North Yemen in the Arab nationalist revolutionary wave, these were not cases of affiliate revolutions disaffiliating with a central revolution, but of loyal affiliate revolutions being abandoned by a central revolution that was in the process of ending its leadership role within the revolutionary wave.

THE COLLAPSE OF THE ARAB NATIONALIST AND MARXIST-LENINIST REVOLUTIONARY WAVES

The collapse of the Arab nationalist and Marxist-Leninist revolutionary waves took place in different ways, but they experienced three traits in common: 1) the renunciation of the central revolutionary role by the state that had played it and the failure of any other regime within the wave to successfully replace it; 2) a desperate struggle for survival on the part of the embattled affiliate revolutions abandoned by the central revolutions upon which they had depended for security assistance; and 3) the general decomposition of these waves.

Waves without Centers

In the Arab nationalist revolutionary wave, Egypt never again played the role of central revolution after its defeat in the 1967 Arab-Israeli War and the withdrawal of its troops from North Yemen later that year. 'Abd al-Nasir appeared to have nothing to do with the coups d'etat that brought Arab nationalist regimes to power in Sudan and Libya in 1969 (the last two Arab nationalist revolutions to occur). Indeed, although in 1967 'Abd al-Nasir had vigorously opposed the "Islamic Pact" proposed by Saudi Arabia, his willingness to join the Organization of the Islamic Conference in 1969 signaled his reconciliation with the conservative Arab monarchies he had long opposed (Haddad 1992, 268). After 'Abd al-Nasir's death in 1970, his successor, Anwar Sadat, further signaled the abandonment of Arab nationalist goals by changing the country's official name from the United Arab Republic (which Cairo had continued to use even after the Syrian secession) to the Arab Republic of Egypt in 1971. In 1972, Sadat expelled the large number of Soviet military advisers 'Abd al-Nasir had allowed into the country, and became increasingly allied with the United States after the 1973 Arab-Israeli War.

Indeed, Sadat totally renounced Arab nationalist goals when he signed the 1978 Camp David Peace Accords with Israel. Under these agreements, which the United States was instrumental in negotiating, peace and diplomatic relations were established between the two former enemies, and the Sinai Peninsula was returned to Egypt. Conservative and radical Arab regimes alike were infuriated with Sadat since the agreement did not involve Israeli withdrawal from other Arab territories that it had occupied in 1967 or the creation of an independent Palestinian state. After the assassination of Sadat in 1981 (not by an Arab nationalist opposition group, but an Islamic fundamentalist one), his successor Hosni Mubarak continued Sadat's unrevolutionary policies of remaining allied to the United States and committed to the Camp David Accords, though in a less flamboyant manner than his predecessor (Hourani 1991, 410-11; Ajami 1992, 160-63).

Syria, Iraq, and, after the emergence of al-Qadhafi in 1969, Libya all attempted to replace Egypt in the role of central revolution, but none succeeded. Syria remained a self-consciously revolutionary regime, but its credentials to lead the Arab nationalist wave were also tarnished by the 1967 defeat. The Syrian Ba'th party's brand of Arab nationalism never succeeded in attracting much of a following elsewhere in the Arab world, due not only to the defeat but also to the increasing perception that the party was simply a smoke screen for Syria's 'Alawite minority, which had come to dominate the army (Batatu 1983, 9-10) to maintain control over the country's Sunni majority. Syria was also increasingly seen as being less interested in helping the Palestinian revolutionaries achieve their goals vis-à-vis Israel than in controlling them itself. Al-Qadhafi attempted to recreate something akin to the United Arab Republic through his much heralded "unions" with other Arab states. The motive for these other states going along with al-Qadhafi, though, seems to have been the desire to obtain money from him. None, however, was willing to allow al-Qadhafi any role in their internal affairs, and so these projects all foundered.

The most serious bid to replace Egypt in the role of central revolution came from Saddam Hussein of Iraq. Because Iraq did not border Israel, the 1967 Arab defeat was not nearly as much a defeat for Iraq as it was for Egypt and Syria. But Saddam Hussein suffered his own defeats when his 1980 attack on Iran failed and his 1990 invasion of Kuwait was rolled back in 1991. Still, the strong public support for Saddam Hussein that welled up in many Arab countries after his invasion of Kuwait showed that he might have had the potential to revive and lead the Arab nationalist revolutionary wave if his forces had not been driven out of that country and humiliatingly defeated by the U.S.-led coalition.

In the Marxist-Leninist revolutionary wave, not only did the USSR stop playing the role of central revolution when it refused to uphold the collapsing subordinate regimes in Eastern Europe, but the USSR itself collapsed at the end of 1991. Unlike the Arab nationalist wave, the Marxist-Leninist wave had no other regime within it that attempted to replace the USSR as the central revolution. As Marxist-Leninist regimes were collapsing in Eastern Europe during the autumn of 1989, though, a last-ditch attempt to seize power was launched by the aspiring Marxist-Leninist revolutionaries in El Salvador (Garcia 1990, 12). The defeat of this effort, as well as the electoral defeat suffered by the Sandinistas in Nicaragua in March 1990; the decline of Soviet aid to Cuba; and the mounting economic crisis in Cuba all brought an end to any prospect that a Latin American resurgence of the Marxist-Leninist revolutionary wave would survive the wave's collapse everywhere else.

The Fate of Revolutionary Regimes

As the two revolutionary waves collapsed, the regimes that composed them pursued one of four different paths: 1) the revolutionary regime was replaced by another type of regime; 2) the regime abandoned the wave's internationalist ideology in favor of another one, though essentially the same people remained in power; 3) the regime claimed to remain faithful to the wave's internationalist ideology, but in fact became nonrevolutionary; and 4) the regime not only remained loyal to the internationalist ideology, but continued to pursue revolutionary goals, albeit unsuccessfully.

Of the seven revolutionary regimes in the Arab nationalist wave, Egypt came closest to abandoning the wave's ideology when it signed the Camp David Accords with Israel. Algeria, North Yemen, and Sudan were avowedly Arab nationalist, but in fact became nonrevolutionary in their foreign policy. Syria, Iraq, and Libya all sought at various times to promote revolutionary goals abroad, but did not succeed. Despite the collapse of the wave in 1967, no Arab nationalist regime was replaced by another type of regime until the case of Sudan in 1985. All the rest remain in power.

Although it has occurred much more recently, the collapse of the Marxist-Leninist revolutionary wave has witnessed a far greater proportion of its constituent regimes being replaced by other types of regimes. Of the twenty-seven Marxist-Leninist regimes in existence at the beginning of 1989, twenty of them were replaced by another type of regime, and almost all of these replacements occurred by the end of 1991. Four of these did not remain intact, but split apart—Czechoslovakia and Ethiopia into two states each, Yugoslavia into five, and the USSR into fifteen. Two others, East Germany and South Yemen, merged with more-populous neighboring states.

Of the seven regimes that were not replaced, two (Angola and Mozambique) formally abandoned Marxist-Leninist ideology, although the same party remained in power. Three others (China, Vietnam, and Laos) remained avowedly Marxist-Leninist, but in fact became nonrevolutionary, both in their foreign policy and in their domestic economic policy. Only two, Cuba and North Korea, remained committed to revolutionary goals, but even these retreated from pursuing them internationally.

Because a far greater proportion of Marxist-Leninist regimes has been replaced compared to Arab nationalist ones, it may appear that the Marxist-Leninist wave has collapsed far more profoundly than the Arab nationalist wave did. It must be noted, though, that Marxist-Leninist leaders and parties that have transformed themselves to a greater or lesser degree have continued to play an important political role in many of the new governments that replaced Marxist-Leninist ones. In several states (including Lithuania, Poland, and Hungary), where democracy replaced Marxist-Leninist regimes, formerly Marxist-Leninist parties were actually elected to office following public disillusionment with the anti-Marxist-Leninist parties that first came to power following the downfall of the old regime. In some of the successor regimes created by the breakup of the USSR or Yugoslavia (including Serbia, Azerbaijan, Georgia, Uzbekistan, Turkmenistan, and Tajikistan), Marxist-Leninists have adopted nationalist or ultranationalist platforms and continue to rule dictatorially. In Russia, the leaders of most of the various political parties, including democratic ones, that have emerged are former Marxist-Leninists. Marxist-Leninist leaders have also been able to remain in power or at least share power in many of the affiliate regimes that were strongly dependent on the USSR for security assistance and that Moscow cut off in the process of abandoning its central revolutionary role. How this feat was managed deserves special attention.

It was noted in the previous chapter that those revolutionary regimes that maintained a lasting voluntary affiliation with the central revolution were those that needed and received substantial security assistance from it. An important element in states giving up the role of central revolution was the need to end the costly security assistance that they had provided to these embattled affiliate regimes. Unlike other examples of disaffiliation and rivalry that had been initiated by erstwhile affiliates before the collapse of the wave, these lasting affiliations were ended by the central revolution.

When they were abandoned, these embattled affiliate regimes entered crises similar to the ones faced by the subordinate revolutions in Eastern Europe after Gorbachev signalled that Moscow would not defend them. But unlike the subordinate revolutions of Eastern Europe, which did not long resist on their own the urban revolutions that rose up against them in 1989, the embattled affiliate regimes made a concerted effort to retain power. To a surprising extent, they have succeeded.

In the Arab nationalist revolutionary wave, Egypt had only one embattled affiliate (North Yemen) when it gave up the role of central revolution. The North Yemeni case is instructive because it was the first example of how an embattled affiliate revolution dependent on a central revolution for military assistance managed to survive the cutoff of military assistance.

As Egyptian forces withdrew from North Yemen in 1967, the collapse of the revolutionary regime there was widely expected. With crucial assistance from the USSR, the republicans were able to thwart a major royalist offensive that occurred shortly after the Egyptian departure. More importantly, seeing no other long-term option, the Yemeni republicans entered a reconciliation process with the royalists and Saudi Arabia (Gause 1990, 75-82). The civil war came to an end in 1970 with the republican regime intact but financially dependent on conservative Saudi Arabia for the next two decades.

As Moscow abandoned the role of central revolution more than two decades after Cairo had, embattled Third World Marxist-Leninist regimes facing an arms cutoff from Russia adopted a course of action similar to North Yemen's after the departure of the Egyptians: they sought improved relations with their previous external foes in order to halt assistance to their internal opponents and to arrange for a peace settlement.

Mozambique first attempted to adopt this strategy several years before the collapse of the Marxist-Leninist revolutionary wave. Unlike Afghanistan, Cambodia, Angola, and Ethiopia, which all received massive military aid from other Marxist-Leninist regimes, Mozambique received only limited assistance from the USSR and its allies in its struggle against South African–backed RENAMO. Mozambique responded not only by seeking military assistance from Britain and Portugal, but by signing the Nkomati Accords with South Africa in 1984. The white minority regime in South Africa, however, continued to arm RENAMO even after it had pledged not to in the Nkomati Accords, and so the war continued (Rubinstein 1988, 163-64; Hume 1994, 11-12).

Later, as the Marxist-Leninist wave was collapsing, Angola, Mozambique, and Cambodia all pursued this strategy successfully. One common feature of these three cases was that their Marxist-Leninist ruling parties formally abandoned Marxism-Leninism and embraced democracy (though their commitment to it was not nearly as great as that of the transformed Marxist-Leninist parties in most East European countries). A second common feature was that their principal internal opponents were regarded as undesirable by most external powers, who cut back or eliminated their assistance to them. UNITA's external support virtually disappeared as the result of three factors: 1) the withdrawal of South Africa from neighboring Namibia (via which Pretoria had previously aided UNITA) and the emergence there of a government friendly to the MPLA; 2) the end of American assistance to UNITA and the recognition of the MPLA government by the Clinton administration shortly after taking office; and 3) the political transformation in South Africa that resulted in the election of a black majority government with no interest in supporting a group that had been backed by the white minority regime it replaced. With ever decreasing external support, UNITA was unable to defeat the MPLA government (an effort that was interrupted temporarily in 1990-91, when UNITA leader Jonas Savimbi thought he would win the UN-supervised elections, but resumed with a vengeance when he lost them until spring 1995, when Savimbi acknowledged MPLA leader dos Santos as Angola's legitimate president).[2]

The political transformation in South Africa also brought an end to external support for RENAMO in Mozambique and an end to the civil war there. UN-supervised elections were also won by the ruling party (Hume 1994; Lloyd 1995). In Cambodia, the unwillingness of the Khmer Rouge to accept electoral defeat in UN-sponsored elections and their resumption of military operations led to increasing international support for the coalition between the former Marxist-Leninists (whose regime Vietnam was no longer willing to protect after Hanoi withdrew its forces in September 1989) and the non-Marxist forces, led by Prince Sihanouk, which had previously been allied with the Khmer Rouge against them (*Strategic Survey 1993-1994*, 176-78; *Strategic Survey 1994-1995*, 188-90).

By contrast, the embattled Marxist-Leninist affiliate regimes in Afghanistan, Nicaragua, South Yemen, and Ethiopia did not survive. But even in some of these cases, their record was not one of complete failure.

The Marxist-Leninist regime in Afghanistan tried to pursue a strategy similar to the one adopted by North Yemen, Angola, Mozambique, and Cambodia. The Afghan Marxist-Leninist regime did indeed survive for over three years after the Soviet troop withdrawal was completed. Many nations, including the United States, had supported the mujahadin groups during the Soviet occupation. This aid was reduced after the Soviet troop withdrawal. Relations between several mujahadin groups and many of their external supporters (including the United States and Saudi Arabia) were ruptured in 1990 when the former voiced support for Saddam Hussein's invasion of Kuwait. Although the various mujahadin groups slowly gained ground against it, they did not overthrow the Marxist-Leninist regime on their own. Its downfall came about only when one of the regime's leading military figures withdrew his support and allied with one of the rival mujahadin factions (*Strategic Survey 1992-1993*, 175-77). Thus, while the Marxist-Leninist regime in Afghanistan was overthrown in 1992, it was not replaced just by its opponents, but by a coalition of some of the mujahadin and an important part of the old regime. This new hybrid regime, however, would lose control of most of Afghanistan, including the capital, to a purely Islamic fundamentalist group in 1996.

In Nicaragua, the Sandinistas were unsuccessful in the sense that they, much to their surprise, lost the March 1990 elections to the democratic opposition. They did, however, remain a potent force in Nicaraguan politics when the newly elected president, Violetta Chamorro, retained one of the leading Sandinista figures, Humberto Ortega, as defense minister. The Sandinistas have maintained a dominant role in the Nicaraguan military and security services ever since.[3] They also have the possibility of returning to power via the ballot box, as their strong second place finish in the 1996 elections demonstrated.[4]

Although the regime in South Yemen did not face an armed insurgency like so many other Third World Marxist-Leninist regimes, it was internally divided and generally unpopular. In order to avoid being overthrown altogether, its leadership accepted the position of coalition partner with the Arab nationalist regime in the North in the united Yemen that came into being peacefully in May 1990. The two ruling parties, however, continued to run the North and South separately, each keeping its own army intact. Increasing tension between the leaderships of the two parties led to the outbreak of civil war in 1994, at which point an attempt by the South to reestablish its independence was defeated by the North. The role of the former Marxist-Leninists in Yemeni politics was thus eliminated. They did, however, play an important role in governing united Yemen for almost four years, between unity in 1990 and the outbreak of war in 1994 (Hudson 1995; Katz 1995b).

The opposition to the Marxist-Leninist regime in Ethiopia had received no support from the United States and the West and very little external assistance from other (mainly Arab) countries. There were, thus, no major powers to which Addis Ababa could appeal to stop supporting its internal opponents who were able to defeat the regime's demoralized forces soon after the Soviet aid cutoff. Of all the embattled affiliate Marxist-Leninist regimes, Ethiopia's collapsed most thoroughly without any element of the old regime being able to play a role in the new one (*Africa South of the Sahara* 1994, 355-56).

Two other Marxist-Leninist regimes—Vietnam and Cuba—had also maintained lasting affiliations with Moscow. Although they did not face insurgencies within their own borders like the others did, they had depended heavily on the USSR for security assistance (primarily vis-à-vis the United States for Cuba, and vis-à-vis China and its Khmer Rouge allies for Vietnam). Unlike most other affiliate Marxist-Leninist regimes in the Third World, these two had also received substantial economic assistance from the USSR. By the time the USSR broke up in 1991, its security and economic assistance to both Havana and Hanoi had been drastically reduced. Since then, the avowedly Marxist-Leninist regimes in both countries have remained in power, but both have responded to this crisis by attempting (as have other embattled affiliate revolutions) to improve their relations with the United States and with the West in general.

Vietnam, though, has been considerably more successful in this effort than Cuba. In 1986, Vietnam began to follow China's economic reform model, in which a Marxist-Leninist regime oversaw a transition from socialism to capitalism in the economic sphere but resisted political reform that would dilute the Marxist-Leninist regime's monopoly on power.

Especially after the Vietnamese withdrawal from Cambodia in 1989, economic ties sprang up between Hanoi on the one hand and Southeast Asia and the West on the other. Despite lingering domestic concerns in the United States over unaccounted-for American MIAs in Vietnam, Washington and Hanoi established diplomatic relations in August 1995.[5]

Cuba has ended its support for revolution abroad, but unlike Vietnam, it has been largely unsuccessful in its effort to lift the American economic embargo and normalize relations with the United States generally. Castro, though, has normalized Cuba's relations with Western Europe and Latin America where governments no longer see him as a threat (some never did). The reason for Washington's continued hostility toward the Castro regime appears not to be related to any perceived threat that it now poses to American interests but instead to the dynamics of American domestic politics, particularly the political strength of the anti-Castro wing of the Cuban-American community.[6]

North Korea (which began its life as a subordinate revolution but gradually asserted its independence and became an affiliate revolution, though one dependent on the USSR for security assistance) was also faced with a crisis when Moscow basically ended the security and economic assistance it had been providing to Pyongyang. North Korea has continued to uphold Marxist-Leninist revolutionary ideology not only rhetorically, but in practice as well. Unlike China or Vietnam, it has made very little progress so far in transforming its economy. More ominously, North Korea's huge army, nuclear weapons program, and bellicose rhetoric have resulted in fears that Pyongyang still harbors ambitions to export its revolution to South Korea by force (Lee 1993, 424-25). Yet North Korea has also sought to improve its relations with the West, especially the United States. Ironically, while North Korea now threatens American interests to a far greater degree than Cuba does, Pyongyang has been more successful than Cuba in obtaining economic assistance from Washington. In 1994, the United States agreed to provide an aid package to North Korea in exchange for the latter halting its nuclear weapons program (*Strategic Survey 1994-95,* 180-83). Still, this rapprochement between the United States and North Korea seems highly unstable, and the possibility of renewed conflict on the Korean Peninsula remains present. By contrast, although relations between Cuba and the United States are poor, they are far more stable in the sense that conflict between them seems highly unlikely.

With few exceptions, then, affiliate revolutionary regimes that had been heavily dependent on a central revolution for security assistance managed to survive the severance of military assistance from the central revolution that occurred as part of the collapse of the revolutionary wave. This was an especially noteworthy feat in the Marxist-Leninist wave where many seemingly weak embattled affiliate regimes survived even though the USSR itself did not.

Their ability to survive resulted from their willingness (indeed, desperation) to be reconciled with most (if not all) of the status quo nations they had previously regarded as enemies. Equally important, the status quo nations were either willing to be reconciled with them or, if not, were unwilling to take concerted effort themselves to oust them. For once these nations were no longer part of an expanding nondemocratic revolutionary wave, and to the extent that they ended their efforts to promote revolution abroad, they were no longer a threat to the status quo, and thus were generally accepted by it.

The Islamic Fundamentalist Wave: Prospects for Collapse

What is the likelihood that the Islamic fundamentalist revolutionary wave will collapse? Despite concern on the part of Western governments and media over the prospect that it will expand, a growing number of scholars are predicting this wave's ultimate collapse. Some of these predictions focus on Iran, the central revolutionary regime within the Islamic fundamentalist wave. According to Laurent Lamote, "Popular support for the Islamic republic is being eroded, and the republic's legitimacy undermined. . . . All available information indicates that the state apparatus is at a loss: it knows it is heading for a crisis that could be fatal to it, but it is unable to make the necessary decisions" (1994, 24). Fred Halliday predicted that the Islamic revolutionary experiment in Iran might come to an end "in a way roughly comparable to what had happened in the communist countries" (1994, 326).

The predictions of other scholars have focused on the Islamic revolutionary wave as a whole. Nazih Ayubi indicated that the expansion of the Islamic fundamentalist revolutionary wave will in the end lead to its collapse when he wrote, "the more Irans and Sudans you get, the less impressive and appealing the Islamists' call will become" (1991, 238). All of Olivier Roy's book, *The Failure of Political Islam,* is devoted to arguing that the Islamic fundamentalist revolutionary wave must collapse because of the intellectual bankruptcy of its political and economic ideas. According to Roy, "The Islamic revolution, the Islamic state, the Islamic economy are myths . . . The coming to power of movements such as the FIS will only make more apparent the emptiness of the phantasm of the 'Islamic state'" (1994, 27).

There can be no guarantee, of course, whether these predictions are accurate, or, if they are, when they will be fulfilled. Should a collapse actually occur, the events leading up to it are likely to be as idiosyncratic, and hence unpredictable, as were the events leading to the collapse of the Arab nationalist and Marxist-Leninist waves. To what extent, though, are the conditions leading up to the collapse of these two earlier revolutionary waves—especially the decision by the leaders of the central revolutionary state to give up this role—present in the Islamic fundamentalist revolutionary wave?

It was noted previously that there were four general preceding conditions present in the central revolution of both the Arab nationalist and the Marxist-Leninist waves before their collapse: economic failure, military stalemate with states outside the revolutionary wave, rivalry within the revolutionary wave, and a general loss of faith in the revolutionary ideology in the states where revolution had occurred. Three of these four general preceding conditions have emerged in the central revolution of the Islamic fundamentalist wave.

Despite its enormous oil reserves, Iran has faced increasing economic problems since its revolution. The basic problem, as Nora Boustany explained, is that "Iran's population has swelled from 30 million to 60 million since the 1979 revolution, while oil revenue has plummeted almost to one-third what it was."[7] In addition to a high level of defense expenditures, especially during the 1980-88 Iran-Iraq War, the populist economic policies which the regime instituted shortly after coming to power has been a large drain on Iran's resources. By one estimate, the level of economic subsidies provided by the Iranian government exactly equals Iran's oil revenues.[8] According to Karshenas and Pesaran,

> The Islamic republic's response to these unfolding economic crises was to follow a policy of severe import compression, international economic isolation, and reliance on bureaucratic arrangements as principal allocative and distributive mechanisms in the economy. The outcome has been a deteriorating economy, rising inflation, foreign indebtedness on an unprecedented scale, a substantial increase in rent-seeking activities at the expense of productive enterprise, a shrinking of capital stock, an inadequately trained work force, and economic institutions that are badly in need of fundamental reform (1995, 89).

They further warn that it will be extremely difficult for the government to institute reform since the distortions caused by its populist policies are so well-entrenched that "their removal, even if gradual, cannot be achieved without initially causing major social and economic dislocations" (105).

Iran has also experienced a dual military stalemate with states outside the Islamic revolutionary wave. First, although Tehran succeeded in pushing Iraqi forces out of most of the Iranian territory they occupied relatively early on in the Iran-Iraq War, the Islamic republic failed to bring about the downfall of Saddam Hussein—which was one of the conditions that Ayatollah Khomeini declared must be fulfilled for Iran to end the war. After many years of failing to defeat Saddam Hussein's forces on Iraqi territory at an enormous cost in terms of Iranian lives, Khomeini finally agreed to end the war without having achieved this goal (Hooglund 1990).

Second, even after the Iran-Iraq War, Iran can be described as being in a military stalemate with other powers in the Persian Gulf region as well as with the United States. After Iran spent about 20 percent of its GDP on the military during the Iran-Iraq War, Tehran has continued to devote a very high proportion of its GDP (variously estimated from 10 to 15 percent) to defense, notwithstanding the country's dire economic problems (Cordesman 1994, 37). Yet despite this effort, Iran is now in a weaker military position vis-à-vis its two main regional rivals than it was under the Shah. As Shahram Chubin wrote, "Compared to its inventory in 1979, Iran today has fewer aircraft, ships, tanks, and helicopters. Its relative position in the region is weaker as Saudi Arabia has modernized and expanded its forces, while even Iraq *after* Desert Storm is still stronger than Iran, compared to its much weaker position numerically and qualitatively in 1979" (1994, 73).

Third, there have been increasing signs of a loss of faith in the Islamic fundamentalist revolutionary ideology among the Iranian populace. One such sign has been the occurrence of antigovernment protest in a number of Iranian cities during the 1990s.[9] Further, there have been reports that officers within the Iranian armed forces, including the Revolutionary Guard, have signalled their unwillingness to "order their troops into battle to quell civil disorder."[10] Another sign of the loss of faith in the regime's ideology is the increasing popularity within Iran of an alternative ideology—Islamic democracy—advocated by the Islamic philosopher, Abdol Karim Soroush.[11] Patrick Clawson noted that while there is "no credible challenge from any opposition force" to the Islamic republic, "There is no important social group that would come to the defense of this regime were it threatened, nor does the regime have the support of a repressive apparatus that can keep it in power against popular discontent" (1994, 47).

Rivalry within the revolutionary wave is the condition present in the Arab nationalist and Marxist-Leninist waves that has not yet become an important factor in the Islamic fundamentalist one. Although Iran did not enjoy a close affiliation with the first Islamic revolutionary regime in Afghanistan, serious rivalry between them did not occur. Iran and Sudan, by contrast, are closely affiliated.

That active rivalry has not yet erupted within the Islamic fundamentalist wave is probably not because Islamic fundamentalist regimes are somehow more virtuous or cooperative with one another than Arab nationalist or Marxist-Leninist regimes were but because there have been so few successful revolutions within the Islamic fundamentalist wave so far. The more Islamic fundamentalist regimes that come to power, it was argued earlier, the more likely it is that rivalry will occur within this wave. The poor relations between Iran and the Taliban forces that captured much of Afghanistan in 1996 indicate that such rivalry may be developing between these two Islamic fundamentalist regimes.[12]

Despite the low level of rivalry among its constituent revolutionary regimes so far, the fact that the Islamic revolutionary wave—and its central revolution in particular—is experiencing three of the four general preceding conditions present before the collapse of the Arab nationalist and Marxist-Leninist waves indicates that the Islamic fundamentalist wave is also vulnerable. But, as was already pointed out, the presence of all four general preceding conditions in these two earlier revolutionary waves did not automatically bring about their collapse; they were able to survive for a long time despite them. Their presence, however, did limit Egypt's and the USSR's choices when they experienced the crisis that led them each in turn to abandon the role of central revolution.

Earlier in this chapter, I argued that there were two elements to the crisis that led to the collapse of the Arab nationalist and Marxist-Leninist waves: 1) overoptimism about the weakness of status quo opponents as well as competition with rival revolutionary regimes that led the central revolution to become involved in military ventures that were unsuccessful and that added significantly to its burdens; and 2) the loss of confidence on the part of the top leadership of the central revolution concerning not only its ability to lead the revolutionary wave, but about the desirability of doing so. It was at this point that the leadership of the Egyptian and Soviet central revolutions respectively decided to abandon military support for embattled affiliate revolutions in return for cooperation and assistance from their once-reviled status quo opponents.

Will the Islamic fundamentalist wave experience a similar crisis? If it does, this appears to be a long way off since the three elements leading to the collapse of the Arab nationalist and Marxist-Leninist waves are either not present or only present to a limited degree in it. While Iran is in a military stalemate with its regional rivals and the United States, it does not have the additional burden of defending embattled affiliate revolutions as Egypt did in North Yemen, or as the USSR and its allies did in several Third World countries. Although the affiliate Islamic fundamentalist regime in Sudan is embattled, Iran has only provided limited military assistance in the form of arms shipments and possibly as many as 2,000 Revolutionary Guards as military advisers (Cordesman 1994, 34-35). If Iran gave any assistance to the embattled Rabbani regime, it was obviously not effective in preventing the Taliban from ousting it from Kabul in 1996.

The one active conflict (the Iran-Iraq war) that Iran did experience military stalemate in was a failed effort to establish a revolutionary regime closely affiliated with (or even subordinate to) Tehran, not to defend an existing one.

There is some evidence of a loss of confidence in elements of Khomeini's Islamic fundamentalist ideology within the ranks of the Iranian clergy: "'Large numbers of clerics are now against the clergy in power. They now think it was a mistake to take government office.'"[13] The very top Iranian clerical leadership, however, has not lost confidence in the Khomeinist insistence on clerical control of the government. There has been a struggle within the leadership between those clerics who advocate continued clerical control over the economy and those, like President Rafsanjani, who have advocated free-market reforms. But as Ervand Abrahamian has pointed out, the defense of private property in the economic sphere actually serves to justify authoritarianism in the political sphere in Khomeinist political thought (1993, 43-45).[14]

Similarly, while Khomeini's successors have pursued a much more conciliatory policy vis-à-vis the West (though not the United States), this does not mean that they have ended Iranian support for aspiring Islamic revolutionaries elsewhere. Indeed, continued pursuit of a revolutionary foreign policy is apparently seen by the top Iranian leadership as helping legitimize the Islamic republic domestically. As Shahram Chubin has argued, Tehran "seeks to affirm the model of its revolution by seeing its adoption elsewhere" (1994, 68).

Finally, since Iran is not heavily involved in the defense of any embattled affiliate revolutions, there are none that can be negatively affected
by an Iranian decision to abandon them. Although Sudan has been unable
to defeat its non-Muslim opponents in the South with the modest amount
of military assistance Tehran provides to Khartoum, the withdrawal of this
Iranian assistance would probably not affect the ability of Sudan's Islamic
fundamentalist regime to contain the rebellion against it. The question,
though, is moot since Iran does not appear at all likely to end its military
aid to Sudan in exchange for improved ties with the West at present.

It is possible, of course, that Iran will become bogged down in defending embattled affiliate Islamic fundamentalist revolutionary regimes
in the future. But the question of whether it may will not arise until additional Islamic fundamentalist regimes come to power, find themselves
embattled, and seek significant military assistance from Iran. Even if all
these contingencies occur (and it is by no means certain that they will), it
is not clear that the Iranian leadership would be willing—or able—to become heavily involved in defending embattled affiliate regimes. The experience of the Iran-Iraq War may have made Tehran wary about undertaking
further military adventures, as its failure to take any significant action in
defense of the embattled Islamic/democratic regime that briefly existed in
Tajikistan in 1992 suggests. On the other hand, the rise of several affiliate
Islamic revolutionary regimes that turn to Tehran for support may lead to
the sort of overoptimism about the weakness of its status quo opponents
that induced Cairo and Moscow to become involved in unsuccessful military ventures that added significantly to their burdens.

If the Islamic fundamentalist revolutionary wave is going to collapse
in the same way as the Arab nationalist and Marxist-Leninist ones did, it
must first expand significantly before it can experience the type of crisis
that would lead to the central revolution abandoning this role.

There is no guarantee, of course, that the Islamic fundamentalist revolutionary wave will experience this type of crisis. Indeed, given the serious
problems that it is experiencing, there is a distinct possibility that the Iranian revolutionary regime will collapse, or somehow become derevolutionized, before the occurrence of many more—perhaps even *any* more—Islamic
fundamentalist revolutions.

How would such a development affect the Islamic fundamentalist wave
as a whole? Just as the emergence of an Islamic fundamentalist regime in
Iran served to inspire and energize Islamic fundamentalists elsewhere, the
downfall of this regime, or even its abandonment of revolutionary goals in

exchange for an alliance with the status quo powers, would surely have a disheartening effect on other Islamic fundamentalists. Neither development, however, would necessarily bring about an end to the Islamic revolutionary wave.

As was noted before, the Islamic fundamentalist wave more closely resembles the Arab nationalist wave in that the disparity in military and economic strength among the countries belonging to them (and which might yet join the Islamic fundamentalist one) are much less than in the Marxist-Leninist wave in which there was a huge such disparity between the USSR on the one hand and all other Marxist-Leninist regimes (except China) on the other. While most Marxist-Leninist regimes (including the one in the USSR itself) did not long survive Moscow's 1989 decision to abandon the role of central revolution, Cairo's 1967 decision to abandon this role did not have a similar effect on Arab nationalist regimes. Indeed, as has been noted before, Arab nationalist revolutions took place in Sudan and Libya two years after Egypt abandoned this role. Arab nationalist regimes in other countries were less dependent on Egypt for their survival than most Marxist-Leninist ones were on the USSR.

It is entirely conceivable, then, that the derevolutionization, or even the downfall, of the Islamic fundamentalist regime in Iran would not necessarily lead to the downfall of the Islamic fundamentalist regimes in Sudan and Afghanistan (which do not appear to be dependent on Tehran for their survival) or even prevent Islamic fundamentalist revolutions elsewhere. Indeed, aspiring Sunni Islamic fundamentalists may not regard the downfall or derevolutionization of the Shi'ite clergy–dominated regime in Tehran as a reason to question the validity of their own revolutionary ideology, but as a vindication of the more intolerant Sunni view of Shi'ism as illegitimate (Roy 1994, 123-24).

But even if the Islamic fundamentalist revolutionary wave survived the downfall or derevolutionization of the regime in Tehran, there are few countries that could play the role of central revolutionary regime more successfully than—or even as successfully as—Iran has played it so far. It is entirely conceivable that an Islamic revolutionary leader as charismatic as Khomeini will lead a successful revolution in a country with a smaller population or fewer resources than Iran. But as the discussion of disaffiliation in chapter 3 indicated, it is highly unlikely that a country with a smaller population or fewer resources than Iran would be acknowledged as the central revolutionary regime by aspiring revolutionaries who came to power elsewhere and were no longer (if they ever were) dependent on it. It is also highly unlikely that such a country would be able—even if its leadership were willing—to long defend an embattled affiliate revolution before experiencing a regime crisis itself.

There are a few predominantly Muslim countries that either surpass or roughly approximate Iran in terms of population: Indonesia, Bangladesh, Pakistan, Turkey, and Egypt. An Islamic fundamentalist revolution in any one of them might serve to inspire the rest of the Islamic world even if Iran withdrew from the Islamic fundamentalist wave. But it is doubtful that any of them would prove to be more capable of playing the role of central revolution (if it chose to play it) than Iran has been. Other Islamic fundamentalist regimes not dependent on its assistance against a strong security threat are unlikely to defer to the state seeking to play the role of central revolution for long, if at all. Islamic fundamentalist regimes in Bangladesh, Pakistan, Egypt, and even Turkey would probably be too poor and weak to defend embattled affiliate revolutions in other countries for long anyway. An Islamic fundamentalist Indonesia, with its population of 191 million and sizeable oil reserves, would be the state most capable of defending embattled affiliate regimes elsewhere. Its geographic isolation from most of the rest of the Islamic world, however, would make this difficult. And much like the former USSR, Indonesia consists of an agglomeration of ethnic groups that were not united voluntarily but by force (Tarling 1966, 47-64, 119-26, 158-77; Low 1991, 302-3; Halperin and Scheffer 1992, 136-37). Involvement in a protracted war to defend an embattled affiliate revolution elsewhere could risk exacerbating ethnic tensions and fueling separatist movements within Indonesia itself.

Of course, Islamic fundamentalist revolution could occur in more than one large state. Because they would not be dependent on each other, this could lead not just to disaffiliation among them, but to rivalry. As with previous revolutionary waves, adherence to a common revolutionary ideology is unlikely to allow its adherents to rise above existing nationalist, ethnic, and even religious (Sunni versus Shi'ite) differences. For example, while Islamic fundamentalists in the Arab world willingly accept material assistance from non-Arab Islamic fundamentalists, the former appear highly unwilling to accept the latter as their leaders. Just as most Islamic fundamentalist movements in the Arab world have been unwilling to subordinate themselves to Iran, it is doubtful that they would be willing to do so to Indonesia, Pakistan, Bangladesh, or Turkey. Indeed, Arab Islamic fundamentalists are especially unlikely to subordinate themselves to an Islamic fundamentalist Turkey (should it ever arise) due to continued Arab bitterness over Ottoman rule. It is also questionable whether an Islamic fundamentalist Egypt would be any more successful in uniting the rest of the Arab world under its leadership than Arab nationalist Egypt was. The country's ideology would change as the result of experiencing a successful Islamic fundamentalist revolution, but its extremely weak economic condition would not.

The history of the Islamic fundamentalist regimes that came to power in Iran, Sudan, and Afghanistan have shown that they are experiencing many of the same—often more intensified—problems plaguing the regimes they replaced: chronic civil war (Sudan and Afghanistan), continuing or increasing poverty (all three), and decreasing legitimacy or even outright opposition stemming from dictatorial rule (all three again). There is little reason to think that other nondemocratic Islamic fundamentalist regimes that come to power will be able to avoid these same problems. Although they may not lead automatically to regime crises, these problems, and the growing disillusion with Islamic fundamentalist regimes that will result from them, will make the Islamic fundamentalist revolutionary wave vulnerable to collapse.

Chapter 5

Status Quo Powers and Revolutionary Waves

The previous three chapters examined the expansion of, affiliation and disaffiliation within, and collapse of revolutionary waves that expand via affiliate revolution. The analysis of these three aspects of revolutionary waves focused on factors internal to them and took little account of the role of the status quo powers. The status quo powers that have opposed them, however, have sought to affect these three aspects of revolutionary waves. Status quo powers have actively sought to prevent revolutionary waves from expanding via affiliate revolutions. They have also sought to take advantage of disaffiliation within revolutionary waves. Finally, they have sought, at least as a long-term goal, the collapse of revolutionary waves. This chapter will assess the impact that the status quo powers have had on these three aspects of revolutionary waves. First, however, something must be said about what constitutes the status quo powers themselves.

With regard to any specific revolutionary wave, the status quo powers are those governments whose interests are threatened by it and that oppose its expansion. Of course, not all status quo powers oppose revolutionary waves as vigorously as others. While many states do not support the expansion of a revolutionary wave, they do little or nothing to prevent it from expanding since they are not strongly threatened and since others have taken upon themselves the burden of countering it anyway. On the other hand, a revolutionary wave is very strongly opposed by governments fighting aspiring revolutionaries within their own borders. In all three revolutionary waves examined here, the leadership of the status quo powers' efforts to counter a revolutionary wave has been undertaken by a major Western state that feels its interests to be particularly threatened by the expansion of the revolutionary wave.

Aside from opposition to revolutionary expansion, however, there have often been important differences among the status quo powers allied against it. The three major Western powers that have played the most important roles in countering revolutionary waves (the United States, the United Kingdom, and France) are three of the most important countries in the democratic revolutionary wave. Many of the Third World countries that were the targets of aspiring revolutionaries, however, were undemocratic regimes of one sort or another (colonies, military dictatorships, absolute monarchies, or others). The status quo powers vis-à-vis revolutionary waves, then, have been coalitions united more by what they are against than by what they are for. This limited congruency of interests has often served to inhibit—sometimes fatally—the extent to which the status quo powers could cooperate with one another against their revolutionary opponents. Nor have the major Western powers always been in agreement on how to respond to revolutionary waves. On the other hand, fear of a new, expanding revolutionary wave has sometimes resulted in previously unthinkable alliances against it, as when once virulently anti-Western Arab nationalist regimes cooperated with the status quo West against the Islamic fundamentalist revolutionary wave that they saw as a common threat. To the extent that they fear being undermined by forces from other revolutionary waves, then, revolutionary states can also become status quo powers.

STATUS QUO POWERS AND ASPIRING REVOLUTIONARIES

The specific threat that the expansion of revolutionary waves poses to the major status quo powers is that a government allied to them will be overthrown and replaced by one allied to their enemy, the central revolutionary state. This threat seems all the more potent due to the possibility that, with its new ally, the central revolutionary state could be in an even stronger position to spread revolution to other states allied to the status quo powers. This fear of "falling dominoes" has served to heighten the importance of countries that may have little value in themselves to the status quo powers but that, allied to the central revolutionary state, they fear would threaten nearby countries with much greater importance to them.

The usual assumption that the leading status quo governments have made in these situations, of course, is that the aspiring revolutionaries threatening their ally are closely affiliated—or even subordinated—to the central revolution and will remain so if they come to power. As has been shown here, however, this assumption has often proven inaccurate. Even when aspiring revolutionaries have been closely allied to the central revolution before coming to power, disaffiliation has frequently occurred afterward. Foreign policymakers operating under "worst case" planning assumptions in the major status quo powers, though, have not been optimistic about this happening. Yet while their pessimism was frequently mistaken, it was certainly understandable in the context of a revolution during which the aspiring revolutionaries and the central revolution proclaimed their undying loyalty toward each other as well as their hostility toward the status quo regime and the West for having supported it.

When the leading Western status quo powers have perceived their Third World allies to be vulnerable to aspiring revolutionaries from a revolutionary wave, their usual response has been to provide their embattled allies with varying degrees of military assistance, ranging from arms transfers to direct military intervention. In the wake of the American experience in Vietnam, counterinsurgency warfare against armed guerrillas (or rural revolution) is now generally regarded as futile for a democracy to undertake. Not all Western counterinsurgency operations, however, were failures. British-sponsored counterinsurgency efforts, for example, defeated aspiring Marxist-Leninist revolutionaries in Greece, Malaya (which later became part of Malaysia), and Oman (Duncanson 1981; Akehurst 1982).

The three major Western powers, though, have all undertaken protracted counterinsurgency efforts that failed: France in Indochina (1945-54) and Algeria (1954-62), the United Kingdom in South Yemen (1964-67), and the United States in Indochina (1964-73). Especially in France and the United States, these protracted counterinsurgency efforts became so unpopular that neither Paris nor Washington has mounted one against aspiring revolutionaries since then. While the British went on to fight a successful counterinsurgency effort in Oman (1965-75) after the debacle in neighboring South Yemen, London has not become involved in fighting an insurgency anywhere else in the Third World since then (though it has fought a low-level campaign against urban guerrillas in Northern Ireland since 1969). Not since the mid-1960s, then, have any of the major Western powers been willing to become heavily involved themselves in new counterinsurgency efforts against aspiring revolutionaries. It seems highly unlikely that this will change.

But if sending their own troops to fight in Third World insurgencies is no longer feasible for the major Western powers, they have pursued an alternative strategy that has often been more acceptable to Western publics: supplying embattled status quo allies with large quantities of arms so that they themselves can fight the aspiring revolutionaries threatening them. This strategy has sometimes proven successful, as shown in the defeat of aspiring Marxist-Leninist revolutionaries in the Philippines and El Salvador in the 1980s, and in Peru in the early 1990s. But Western arms were of little or no value in other cases in which the armies possessing them either could not or would not use them effectively against even poorly armed adversaries, as in Cuba in 1959 and Iran in 1979. And in those cases where revolution occurred through elements within a country's armed forces undertaking a coup d'état (as in Egypt, 1952; Libya, 1969; and Ethiopia, 1974), Western weapons not only failed to hinder the aspiring revolutionaries but, contrary to Western intentions, actually helped them succeed instead.

Thus, while sometimes successful, Western military assistance has often failed to prevent affiliate revolutions. The exact circumstances under which these failures have occurred have been as diverse as the various revolutions that succeeded. There have, however, been certain commonalities in these failures.

First, the major Western status quo governments have been far more concerned with the international consequences of revolution than with its domestic causes. Theda Skocpol observed that "Democracies, we know, even imperfect ones, have rarely been susceptible to either the expansion or the victory of revolutionary movements" (1994, 311). Virtually all of the pro-Western regimes that have succumbed to revolution have either been dictatorships or colonies. Yet the major Western powers, leading democracies themselves, have persisted in supporting nondemocratic regimes in countries where they seek to prevent revolutionary waves from spreading despite the fact that these regimes are more vulnerable to revolution.

There have, of course, been important reasons why the major Western powers have attempted to prevent revolution by supporting nondemocratic regimes. First, since nondemocratic status quo regimes allied to them have been the ones that were vulnerable to revolution, it is the prospect of their being ousted that the major Western powers have faced. Second, as Jeane Kirkpatrick pointed out, it is extremely difficult for a nondemocratic government to undergo a democratic transformation when it "is fighting for its life against violent adversaries" (1979, 44). Third, before the point at which it is "fighting for its life," the typical nondemocratic regime supported by the West has usually been highly unwilling to democratize; its goal is not simply to defeat aspiring revolutionaries affiliated with a nondemocratic revolutionary wave, but to defeat all its opponents, including democratic ones, and remain firmly in control without sacrificing any of its authoritarian power. Fourth, the major Western powers have often feared that nondemocratic revolutionaries would take advantage of elections to come to power democratically but then destroy democracy after being elected. Fifth, efforts at democratization in many artificially created multiethnic states could result—especially under conditions in which ethnic tension is widespread—in a state's violent disintegration, not its peaceful integration.

Despite these risks, the United States did successfully pursue democratization toward the end of the Cold War in the Philippines (1986), South Korea (1987-88), and Chile (1988-90). But, despite their long experience with dictatorial regimes, conditions were nearly ideal in these countries for a peaceful transition to democracy. There existed in all of them strong democratic opposition movements to which power could be transferred. Nondemocratic aspiring revolutionaries were virtually nonexistent in South Korea and were insignificant in Chile. Further, both of these transformations took place at a time when Soviet-American rivalry in the Third World had essentially ended. There was a significant Marxist-Leninist opposition in the Philippines, but this was Maoist and anti-Soviet. Indeed, during the crisis leading up to the American-assisted ouster of Ferdinand Marcos and transfer of power to the democratically elected Corazon Aquino in 1986, the USSR (then still at odds with the United States in the Third World) issued strong statements in support of Marcos, apparently in the hope that he would survive the crisis, end his country's alliance with the United States, and move closer to Moscow (Katz 1990b, 124-26). Finally, there were no strong ethnic tensions or secessionist movements within South Korea or Chile. In the Philippines, by contrast, there was a secessionist movement on the part of the Muslims of Mindinao. While Filipino democratization has been accompanied by the demise of the aspiring Marxist-Leninist New People's Army, which had ambitions to seize power nationally, secessionist movements on Mindinao have persisted (Hutchcroft 1995, 432).

The existence of strong democratic opposition movements, the weakness and/or isolation of the nondemocratic ones, the lack of a connection between the USSR and existing nondemocratic aspiring revolutionaries, and the lack of or weakness of ethnic tensions and secessionist movements all reduced the risk that promoting democratization would lead to the development of a nondemocratic revolutionary regime or the breakup of the country in these three cases. But where democratic opposition movements have been weak, nondemocratic opposition movements have been strong and closely affiliated with a revolutionary wave (or were believed to be), and ethnic tensions or secessionist tendencies strong, the risks of promoting democratization have usually been perceived as too great by the major Western powers.

In those cases in which promoting democratization appeared highly risky, support for the status quo dictatorship has usually been seen by Western governments as comparatively less so. The problem with this policy, however, is that while it may appear less risky to Western governments, it neglects the fact that the known repressiveness of the status quo dictatorship is far more the immediate focus of popular discontent in the country it rules than the unknown possibility that its nondemocratic opponents—who always claim to be democratic—may, once in power, prove to be equally or even more repressive. Further, while the undemocratic status quo regime attempts to suppress both its democratic and nondemocratic opponents, it is the former that can be more readily eliminated if they are either unarmed or less well armed than the nondemocratic ones. If aspiring nondemocratic revolutionaries receive some external support while aspiring democratic ones receive none, then the former are in a stronger position to take over if the regime experiences a crisis that causes it to lose its grip on power.

How such crises came about in status quo regimes varied in different cases, but they often experienced general preceding conditions similar to those discussed in chapter 4 that would in turn confront nondemocratic revolutionary regimes: economic failure, military stalemate, and a general loss of faith in the regime's ideology. One factor that appears to have contributed greatly to regime crises in embattled status quo states is that even though Western governments have usually been willing to give military support to dictatorships, Western public opinion—especially after the bitter experience of unsuccessful counterinsurgency efforts—has placed important constraints on the extent to which they may do so. Domestic politics within a Western state, it has been seen, can force its government to curtail or end its military assistance to an embattled status quo dictatorship. This may either trigger or exacerbate a regime crisis from which the dictatorship cannot recover.

But even such a drastic step may not be necessary to trigger a regime crisis. Henry Munson, for example, has argued that "the most important *precipitating* cause of the Iranian Revolution was the Carter administration's human rights policy, or more precisely, the Iranian perception of that policy" (1988, 126). Munson pointed out that the Carter administration did not end American military support for the Shah, but the Shah's opponents and the Shah himself perceived Carter's human rights policy as signalling the withdrawal of American support for his regime. Indeed, the American public's well publicized unwillingness to support costly U.S. efforts to defend embattled status quo dictatorships in the wake of the American experience in Indochina may have served to embolden nondemocratic aspiring revolutionaries and to precipitate regime crises in the many Third World countries where status quo regimes allied to the United States were overthrown in the 1970s.

While not completely unsuccessful at preventing the expansion of nondemocratic revolutionary waves via affiliate revolution, the major Western powers have clearly failed to achieve this goal universally, as evidenced by all the affiliate Marxist-Leninist, Arab nationalist, and Islamic fundamentalist revolutions that have occurred despite significant Western efforts to prevent them. Expansion via affiliate revolution has proved extremely difficult for the status quo powers to cope with or prevent.

STATUS QUO POWERS AND
DISAFFILIALTION WITHIN REVOLUTIONARY WAVES

As was shown in chapter 3, disaffiliation frequently occurs after aspiring revolutionaries come to power, when differences between them and the central revolution emerge. This disaffiliation is obviously very much in the interests of the major status quo powers to promote. To the extent that revolutionary regimes are closely affiliated with one another, they can more easily work together against the status quo. On the other hand, to the extent that revolutionary regimes have disaffiliated with and are hostile toward one another, they are less able to work together against the status quo.

When the status quo powers fail to prevent the occurrence of affiliate revolution, their motivation to promote disaffiliation between affiliate revolutions and the central revolution after the former come to power would appear to be quite strong. Yet this is something at which the major Western powers have not often succeeded.

This seems to be a virtually impossible task when an affiliate revolutionary regime first comes to power, since there is a mutually reinforcing antagonism that almost always rises up between it and the major status quo powers. Usually, the animosity is mutual right from the start when the new revolutionary regime does exactly what the status quo powers feared by allying closely with the central revolution and pursuing a revolutionary foreign policy. Sometimes, however, a revolutionary regime has sought normal relations as well as aid from the West, but its pursuit of revolutionary foreign-policy goals, as well as Western domestic politics, have prevented this. Hanoi, for example, sought to normalize relations with the United States and even had hopes of obtaining economic assistance from it after the defeat of the Saigon regime in 1975 (Brzezinski 1983, 228-29, 416-17; Rodman 1994, 191). But Hanoi's continued pursuit of revolutionary foreign-policy goals (including close alliance with the USSR, and later, invasion and occupation of Cambodia), as well as American domestic politics (general resentment over the U.S. defeat and specific concerns over the MIA issue), prevented this from happening until long after Hanoi had withdrawn its forces from Cambodia.

On rare occasions, a major status quo power has deliberately attempted to establish good relations with a new revolutionary regime to encourage it to cooperate with the West and not be hostile toward it. This, for example, was the policy of the Carter administration toward the revolutionary regimes that came to power in Nicaragua and Iran in 1979. But the effort proved futile in both cases. The Sandinistas accepted economic assistance from the Carter administration, but at the same time closely affiliated with both Cuba and the USSR while also promoting revolution elsewhere in Central America (Rodman 1994, 226-33). American efforts to befriend the Iranian revolutionary "moderates" seemed to be working during the regime's first nine months in office, but these foundered with the seizure of the American Embassy and the rise of the radicals. Indeed, the radicals were able to make use of the moderates' links with the United States to successfully discredit and oust them (Bakhash 1984, 69-70; Sick 1986, 221-23, 240).

Even when sharp disaffiliation between an affiliate revolution and a central revolution occurs, rapprochement between the new disaffiliate revolution and the status quo powers does not necessarily occur. There were four cases of sharp disaffiliation in the Marxist-Leninist revolutionary wave (Yugoslavia, Albania, China, and Cambodia) and two in the Arab nationalist one (Iraq and Syria). In the Iraqi, Syrian, Albanian, and Cambodian cases, the newly disaffiliate revolutions remained hostile to the status quo powers despite the emergence of extremely hostile relations between them and the central revolution as well as with other revolutionary regimes. In the Chinese case, rapprochement with the United States could only occur a decade after Beijing had disaffiliated with Moscow. In the Yugoslav case alone did rapprochement with the status quo powers and disaffiliation with the central revolution occur at roughly the same time.

In the Iraqi, Syrian, and Chinese cases, the regime did not just disaffiliate with its central revolution, but launched a bid to rival it. So long as they maintained this effort, rapprochement with the status quo was not an important goal for them. It was not until well after its record three disaffiliations (first with Yugoslavia, then the USSR, and finally with China) that Marxist-Leninist Albania sought even a limited rapprochement with the status quo powers (Biberaj 1985, 41-46). The Khmer Rouge in Cambodia did not seek to displace Moscow as the central revolution the way Beijing did, but they were fervently committed to a revolutionary policy and did not seek rapprochement with the status quo powers (Rodman 1994, 183-90). The way Albania and Khmer Rouge–ruled Cambodia responded to the security threat they perceived from neighboring Marxist-Leninist regimes (Yugoslavia and Vietnam, respectively) was to strongly affiliate with more distant revolutionary regimes which with these neighbors had fallen out (first the USSR and then China, in the case of Albania; and China for Khmer Rouge–ruled Cambodia).

It was Tito's independent pursuit of a revolutionary policy (he provided assistance to aspiring Marxist-Leninist revolutionaries in Greece after World War II) that Stalin disliked and that contributed to the Soviet-Yugoslav rupture in 1948. Before then, Tito had shown little sign of desiring rapprochement with the status quo powers. It was because the Soviet-Yugoslav rift posed such a threat to his continued rule in Yugoslavia that Tito sought rapprochement with the West; survival was far more important than the pursuit of revolutionary goals vis-à-vis other countries (Jelavich 1983, 328-29). By contrast, Mao Tse-tung had far less to fear from Khrushchev at the time of the Sino-Soviet rift than Tito had from Stalin a decade earlier. It was only after Sino-Soviet relations had deteriorated to the point of serious clashes along their common frontier that Beijing saw the threat emanating from Moscow to be greater than that posed by Washington. At this point China reduced its support for revolution (Beijing had lost the battle for the loyalty of aspiring Marxist-Leninist revolutionaries in most Third World countries to Moscow by the early 1970s anyway) and sought a de facto alliance with the United States (Garthoff 1985, 199-240).

Compared to revolutions that disaffiliated sharply with a central revolution, affiliate revolutions that either never became strongly affiliated with one or drifted away from it gradually, were, on the whole, more willing to seek rapprochement with the status quo powers. This was true of all six revolutions in this category in the Marxist-Leninist revolutionary wave (Congo, Benin, Guinea-Bissau, Cape Verde, Madagascar, and Mozambique) and two out of the three Arab nationalist revolutions in it (Algeria and Sudan). In all of these cases, rapprochement with the status quo powers was facilitated by these regimes' limited or nonexistent ambitions to spread revolution. By contrast, the one revolution in this category with which rapprochement with the status quo powers did not take place, Libya, was also the one that most ambitiously pursued revolutionary goals, seeking to replace Egypt as the central revolution in a revived Arab nationalist wave.

Finally, no significant rapprochement took place between the status quo powers and those revolutions that remained closely affiliated to the central revolution before the collapse of the revolutionary wave. In chapter 3, it was noted that lasting affiliation between an affiliate revolution and a central revolution only occurs when the former faces a serious security threat against which the latter provides significant military assistance. Affiliate revolutions in which both these conditions were present and in which their affiliation with the central revolution lasted until the collapse of the revolutionary wave were: North Yemen in the Arab nationalist wave; and North Vietnam/Vietnam, Cuba, South Yemen, Ethiopia, Angola, Afghanistan, and Nicaragua in the Marxist-Leninist one. These conditions are also present in Sudan in the Islamic fundamentalist wave.

In most of these cases, the root of the security threat was armed internal opposition, which either sought to overthrow the revolutionary regime (as in North Yemen in the Arab nationalist wave; South Yemen, Angola, Ethiopia, and Nicaragua in the Marxist-Leninist one; and Afghanistan in both the Marxist-Leninist and the Islamic fundamentalist waves), and/or sought to establish a secessionist regime in part of the state (South Yemen and Ethiopia in the Marxist-Leninist wave, and Sudan in the Islamic fundamentalist one). While Hanoi did not face serious internal threats in North Vietnam after the departure of the French, or in Vietnam as a whole after the departure of the Americans, it was involved in conflict with these two major Western powers until 1954 and 1973, respectively. Although faced with no internal threat in Vietnam itself afterward, Hanoi became involved in a major effort to defend the subordinate regime it installed in Cambodia in 1978. Similarly, while Cuba has faced no serious armed internal threat since its revolution and while the American external threat ended in 1962, its government has had hostile relations with the United States from its revolution until the present.

Though not in all cases, the major Western governments contributed to the threat to affiliate revolutionary regimes by providing military assistance to their internal opponents. This was especially true of the United States under Reagan when Washington provided substantial military assistance to the mujahadin in Afghanistan; the contras in Nicaragua; UNITA in Angola; and, to a much lesser extent, two small non-Marxist opposition groups in Cambodia (Knutsen 1992). In 1996, the United States reportedly began providing assistance via Ethiopia, Eritrea, and Uganda to secessionist rebels fighting against the Islamic fundamentalist regime in Sudan.[1]

It might be argued, as it often was during the Cold War, that if the major Western powers had not adopted hostile policies toward these affiliate revolutionary regimes, they would not have feared the West and thus affiliated so closely with their central revolution (Rodman 1994, 284-85). In other words, had they not faced a strong security threat, which was magnified by Western policy, they would have lacked the incentive to seek such a close or long-term affiliation with their central revolution. Instead, they may have disaffiliated or drifted away from the central revolution as did other affiliate revolutions that did not face a strong security threat against which they needed military assistance from the central revolution to fight.

This logic, however, is questionable. In many cases it was not the major Western powers but regional ones that provided most of the military assistance to the internal opponents of embattled affiliate revolutionary regimes. Saudi Arabia provided most of the aid to the royalists in North Yemen and various non-Marxist groups in South Yemen. Although the United States gave military assistance to opposition groups in Angola and Cambodia, more substantial aid was given by the white minority regime in South Africa to UNITA and by China to the Khmer Rouge. In addition to the United States, many states provided military assistance to the Afghan mujahadin, including Iran, Pakistan, Saudi Arabia, and others. But even with virtually no external military assistance to their internal opponents, the insurgencies against embattled affiliate revolutionary regimes would not necessarily have ended. Insurgents fighting the Marxist-Leninist regime in Ethiopia and the Islamic fundamentalist regime in Sudan received little significant external assistance but could not be defeated by revolutionary regimes that did.

In some cases, though, it could be argued that insurgencies against affiliate revolutionary regimes would not have been sustained without military assistance from a major Western power. It is highly doubtful, for example, that the Nicaraguan contras could have sustained their insurgency against the Sandinista regime for as long as they did without American military assistance. Nevertheless, even if the contras had not received American support but instead had been quickly defeated, the Sandinistas still might have felt threatened by the United States and sought lasting affiliation with Cuba and the USSR. Cuba, after all, did not face any serious armed opposition after the 1961 Bay of Pigs operation, and yet it continued to feel threatened by the United States and maintained a lasting affiliation with the USSR despite the important differences that at times arose between Moscow and Havana.

For whether or not they faced an armed insurgency, all the affiliate revolutions that maintained a lasting affiliation with their central revolution actively sought to export revolution. The difference between these affiliate revolutions and rival revolutions was that while the latter sought to promote revolution in competition with the central revolution, the affiliate revolutions did so in cooperation with it, thus making them seem all the more dangerous to the status quo powers.

Whether or not the major status quo powers could have pursued peaceful, nonthreatening relations with these affiliate revolutions while they were actively seeking to promote revolution against regimes allied to the status quo powers, it is understandable why they seldom did so. The risk for a status quo power in pursuing such a policy was that it might not only fail to motivate the affiliate revolution to disaffiliate with its central revolution, but the affiliate revolution might continue its efforts to export revolution despite (indeed, with the help of) any economic or other assistance provided by the status quo power.

This is exactly what happened on the few occasions that the United States attempted a rapprochement with revolutionary regimes that were determined to support the spread of revolution to other countries: Cuba in the mid-1970s, Iran and Nicaragua in the late 1970s, and Iran in the mid-1980s. Soviet-American detente in the 1970s also ended as a result of military intervention on the part of the USSR and two of its stronger affiliate revolutions—Cuba and Vietnam—in support of weak affiliate ones in Angola, Ethiopia, Cambodia, and Afghanistan.

If these embattled affiliate revolutions had not faced strong security threats, they may not have maintained lasting affiliations with their central revolutions, but this does not necessarily mean that they would have sought rapprochement with the status quo powers. They might have become rival revolutions instead, as did other revolutionary regimes that were ambitious to promote revolution and did not need help from the central revolution against a serious security threat.

Whether this would have happened in the Marxist-Leninist or Arab nationalist waves, or might yet happen in an expanded Islamic fundamentalist wave, cannot be stated with certainty. What can be said, however, is that there are serious limits on the ability of status quo powers to promote disaffiliation within a revolutionary wave or to ally with regimes that do disaffiliate. The status quo powers have been most successful at establishing rapprochement with two types of revolutionary regimes: 1) those that do not face strong security threats and are relatively unambitious about exporting revolution; and 2) those that, whether or not they seek to export revolution, face strong security threats, either from the central revolution itself (as in Yugoslavia and China), or from which the central revolution does not protect them (as in Mozambique). On the other hand, status quo powers have had the least success at establishing rapprochement with two other types of revolutionary regime: 1) rival revolutions that seek to promote revolution in competition with the central revolution; and 2) affiliate revolutions that seek to promote revolution in cooperation with the central revolution.

STATUS QUO POWERS AND
THE COLLAPSE OF REVOLUTIONARY WAVES

The status quo powers have had very little success in seeing affiliate revolutionary regimes ousted before the collapse of revolutionary waves. The only Marxist-Leninist regimes that were overthrown before the wave collapsed in 1989-91 were the few such regimes that briefly came to power outside of Soviet Russia in the aftermath of World War I (Hungary, Bavaria, and the "Gilan Soviet" in northwestern Iran); the Azeri and Kurdish Soviet republics in northwestern Iran that had come into being when Soviet troops occupied northern Iran during World War II and that fell soon after their withdrawal in 1946; and Grenada in 1983. No Arab nationalist regime collapsed during the heyday of that wave from 1952 to 1967; since then, only the one in Sudan has been overthrown. In the Islamic fundamentalist revolutionary wave, the Islamic/democratic regime that came to power in Tajikistan in 1992 was ousted later that same year, while the Islamic fundamentalist regime that came to power in Afghanistan in 1992 was displaced in much of the country (including the capital) by another Islamic fundamentalist regime in 1996.

In most of these prewave collapse cases, weak revolutionary regimes were defeated either by the armies of the central government in states where they had taken control of a region (Bavaria and the three Iranian cases) or by external intervention from other states (Hungary, Grenada, and Tajikistan) (Ulam 1974, 426-27; Mawdsley 1987, 124-27; Rodman 1994, 252-53; Zirinsky 1994, 50; Katz 1995a). By contrast, internal opponents rarely succeeded in toppling an affiliate revolutionary regime before the collapse of a revolutionary wave despite receiving military assistance from the status quo powers and others.[2] But by frustrating central revolutionary states' protracted and costly efforts to defeat them, military assistance from the status quo powers to the internal opponents of affiliate revolutions did eventually contribute to the decision by Cairo and Moscow to abandon the role of central revolution and stop defending embattled affiliate revolutions that they no longer viewed as assets but as liabilities.

After they gave up this role, the former central revolutionary regimes experienced rapprochement with the major status quo powers. This process, though, occurred fitfully in both cases. Although Egypt abandoned this role after its defeat in the June 1967 war, rapprochement between Cairo and Washington did not begin in earnest until after the October 1973 war. Rapprochement between Egypt and the conservative Arab states, however, began in 1967 (Kerr 1971, 129-56; Hourani 1991, 419-21). Rapprochement between Washington and Moscow was complicated by the breakup of the USSR in 1991, a development that the Bush administration had hoped to prevent due to the instability it (correctly) foresaw would result.[3] Russian-American relations have cooled since then, but it is no longer the attempt by Moscow to export revolution which divides them.

Abandoned by the central revolution, most of the embattled affiliate revolutions ended what remained of their own efforts to export revolution and sought rapprochement with the major status quo powers in order to induce them to stop providing military assistance to their internal opponents. The status quo powers, in turn, usually responded favorably to such overtures. Saudi Arabia decreased its support for the North Yemeni royalists soon after Egypt withdrew its forces (Stookey 1978, 248-49). Similarly, American support for UNITA in Angola, the mujahadin in

Afghanistan, and the contras in Nicaragua all declined as the Marxist-Leninist wave was collapsing. After pursuing policies that served to strengthen the Khmer Rouge, which was the strongest force opposing the Vietnamese occupation of Cambodia, the United States moved quickly to isolate and weaken them after the Vietnamese withdrew (Knutsen 1992, 201-2). As was pointed out in chapter 4, though, not all embattled affiliate revolutions abandoned by a central revolution survived, despite their efforts to seek rapprochement with the West. But even then, elements of the old regime sometimes managed to make a deal with their adversaries and, regardless of the wishes of the status quo powers, preserve an important role in the new regime, as they did in Nicaragua following the 1990 elections and the emergence of the first Afghan Islamic fundamentalist regime in 1992.

As revolutionary waves collapse, not only do the alliances between a central revolution and its embattled affiliate revolutions come to an end, but the alliances between the status quo powers and the internal opponents of affiliate revolutions either become greatly attenuated or end as well. Sometimes the status quo powers that had been supporting these internal opponents agreed to end their assistance as part of a bargain whereby the central revolution and its other allies agreed to withdraw their forces that had been defending the embattled affiliate revolution. But aid from the status quo powers to the internal opponents of revolutionary regimes usually declined even in the absence of such an agreement.

These alliances, between the major status quo powers and the internal opponents of affiliate revolutionary regimes, were marriages of convenience; their interests were not the same. The status quo powers supported these internal opponents because the enemy regime was part of a revolutionary wave that the West opposed. As long as an affiliate revolution did not attempt to take on the mantle of a central revolution, there was no reason for the status quo powers to fear it after the collapse of a revolutionary wave. And where the internal opponents of this regime were nondemocratic revolutionaries hostile to the West (as were the most powerful mujahadin groups in Afghanistan as well as the Khmer Rouge in Cambodia), the alliance between them and the major Western powers deteriorated quickly once their basic common objective (the withdrawal of foreign armed forces protecting the embattled affiliate revolution) was achieved.

The major Western democratic powers have actively supported democratization of post–wave collapse revolutionary regimes showing a strong domestic impetus for this. But democratization has not occurred in all such states: it has proceeded the farthest in the former subordinate Marxist-Leninist regimes of Eastern Europe and the Baltic states. It has made some, but uneven, progress in certain former Soviet republics, such as Russia, Ukraine, Armenia, and Kyrgyzstan. Little or no progress toward democratization has been made in any of the postrevolutionary Arab nationalist regimes, most of the former affiliate Marxist-Leninist revolutionary regimes in the Third World, or some other former Soviet republics.

Far from insisting upon their democratization, the major Western democratic states have often allied with these nondemocratic postrevolutionary regimes. They have done this for the same reason that they allied (and continue to ally) with nondemocratic status quo governments: the fear that such regimes are vulnerable to being overthrown by aspiring revolutionaries from an expanding revolutionary wave that are hostile to the major Western powers.

Since the Iranian Revolution in 1979, the major Western powers have feared the expansion of the Islamic fundamentalist revolutionary wave. Thus, in addition to supporting nondemocratic status quo governments in the Middle East to prevent the expansion of the Arab nationalist and Marxist-Leninist revolutionary waves, they also came to support nondemocratic postrevolutionary Arab nationalist ones, including Egypt, Algeria, and even Iraq during much of the Iran-Iraq War. Similarly, the fear of Islamic fundamentalism has resulted in the major Western powers acquiescing to Russian support for the nondemocratic Marxist-Leninist regimes in several of the Muslim republics of former Soviet Central Asia, including Uzbekistan, Turkmenistan, Kazakhstan, and Tajikistan.

Ironically, then, the status quo powers now seek to protect these nondemocratic regimes that had previously belonged to revolutionary waves hostile toward them. It is hardly surprising, though, that the major Western democracies prefer nondemocratic regimes that survived the collapse of a revolutionary wave and halted their efforts at spreading revolution, compared to nondemocratic regimes that are part of an active revolutionary wave and are currently attempting to spread it. But the policy of supporting nondemocratic postrevolutionary regimes involves the same risks for the Western democratic states as supporting nondemocratic status quo regimes. By once again focusing on the international consequences of revolution rather than its domestic causes, Western governments fail to pay heed to the fact that it is the known repressiveness of the postrevolutionary dictatorship that is far more the immediate focus of popular discontent than the aspiring revolutionaries fighting against it.

Like many nondemocratic status quo regimes, nondemocratic postrevolutionary ones suppress both their democratic and nondemocratic opponents. If the former receive little or no support while the latter receive some from other revolutionary regimes, it is the latter that may be in a stronger position to take over if the postrevolutionary regime experiences a crisis that causes it to lose its grip on power. While it is not inevitable that this will occur in all countries where the status quo powers are supporting nondemocratic postrevolutionary regimes against aspiring revolutionaries, the evidence suggests that this logic is at work in several important cases.

Following riots that took place in 1988, Algeria's ruling FLN—the Arab nationalist revolutionary regime that came to power when the French withdrew in 1962—began a liberalization process that it thought it could dominate. However, an Islamic party, the FIS, was the primary winner of the local and municipal elections held in June 1990 and of the first round of the national parliamentary elections held in December 1991. A coup d'etat in January 1992, though, brought the army (which had been created by the FLN) to power, and the army soon thereafter banned the FIS. A fierce civil war has taken place since then. While held in check during the period of the FIS's legality from 1989 until 1992, "radical Islam has resurfaced with a vengeance since the 1992 coup" (Entelis 1995, 15).

During the brief period in 1992 when the Islamic/democratic coalition was in power in Tajikistan, the democrats played a major role in the government. Both these groups, however, were forced out of office and into opposition when Russian and Uzbek soldiers reinstated the postrevolutionary, nondemocratic Marxist-Leninist regime that they had ousted. In the civil war that has taken place since then, the Islamic forces have reportedly become increasingly dominant in the opposition movement while the democratic forces have been marginalized (Katz 1995a, 250-55).

In Egypt, the postrevolutionary Mubarak regime initiated limited liberalization in the 1980s, but it has retracted much of this in the 1990s. The Mubarak regime has specifically sought to curtail Islamic opposition groups from operating legally. But while it has been able to accomplish this goal, it has been unable to suppress the growing Islamic fundamentalist insurgency being waged against it by nondemocratic groups. According to one observer, "Since the population is aware that the government cannot be changed by peaceful means, the secular political opposition, which lacks force to change the government, is perceived as marginal" (Cassandra 1995, 18-19).

It is often debated whether Islamic parties would respect democracy if they come to power via electoral means. The principal external supporters of the postrevolutionary non-democratic regimes in these three cases (France vis-à-vis Algeria, Russia vis-à-vis Tajikistan, and the United States vis-à-vis Egypt) have all accepted, though not always publicly, the argument that Islamic parties would quickly destroy democracy if they were allowed to come to power this way. In all three cases, however, the attempt to suppress all opposition to the postrevolutionary nondemocratic regime has served only to strengthen their nondemocratic Islamic fundamentalist opponents vis-à-vis their democratic ones (whether Islamic or not).

Democratization, though, does not necessarily provide immunization against Islamic fundamentalist revolutionaries. In 1989 the Islamic fundamentalist regime that came to power in Sudan did so by ousting the democratic government, which had emerged from the largely peaceful urban revolution of 1985 that disposed of the U.S.-backed postrevolutionary Arab nationalist regime. Sudan's democratic government of the late 1980s suffered from numerous problems that made it especially vulnerable: economic collapse, parliament's inability to modify unpopular measures introduced by the previous government, civil war in the southern part of the country, and lack of foreign support (this government was especially distrustful of the United States, which had supported its nondemocratic predecessor). Despite these problems, though, the fact remains that the Islamic fundamentalist regime in Sudan did come to power by overthrowing a democracy and not a nondemocratic status quo or postrevolutionary regime. Skocpol wrote that democracies "have rarely been susceptible" to revolution—not that they ever were (1994, 311).

Just because Islamic fundamentalist revolutionaries succeeded in overthrowing a democracy in this one instance, however, does not show that democracy is more susceptible than other forms of government to this type of revolution. Islamic fundamentalist revolutionaries have also overthrown a nondemocratic status quo regime in Iran, a Marxist-Leninist regime in Afghanistan, and another Islamic fundamentalist regime in Afghanistan.

CONCLUSION

The major status quo powers attempted to prevent the expansion of the Arab nationalist, Marxist-Leninist, and Islamic fundamentalist revolutionary waves via affiliate revolution. Yet status quo nondemocratic regimes have often succumbed to aspiring revolutionaries from nondemocratic revolutionary waves despite military assistance to them from the major Western democracies. In addition, the major status quo powers have had an interest in promoting and exploiting disaffiliation within revolutionary waves. But when a revolutionary regime continues to promote revolution in other countries even after disaffiliating with a central revolution, rapprochement between it and the status quo powers is unlikely. Further, military assistance from the major status quo powers and their regional allies to the internal opponents of affiliate revolutions only serves to promote their lasting affiliation with the central revolution. And while the status quo powers work for and actually help to bring about the collapse of a revolutionary wave, its occurrence leads to serious problems that they neither anticipate nor deal with adequately. Specifically, the major status quo powers have been willing to ally with most postrevolutionary nondemocratic regimes, provided that they no longer seek to export revolution. But the regimes that survived the collapse of either the Arab nationalist or Marxist-Leninist wave in predominantly Muslim countries are proving vulnerable to aspiring revolutionaries from the Islamic fundamentalist revolutionary wave.

What is remarkable, then, is that the status quo powers have only limited ability, at best, to affect major aspects of nondemocratic revolutionary waves that expand via affiliate revolutions. The success or failure of affiliate revolutions appears less dependent on the quantity of military assistance that embattled status quo regimes receive from the West—or aspiring revolutionaries receive from the central revolution—than on the internal political dynamics within the country experiencing it. Disaffiliation appears less dependent on the diplomacy of the status quo powers than on the breakdown of relations between central and affiliate revolutions. And while the actions of the status quo powers contribute to the collapse of revolutionary waves, what happens to the post–wave collapse revolutionary regimes depends less on the preferences or level of assistance from the status quo powers than on the internal political dynamics of the individual countries that had belonged to the wave.

Just as many Arab nationalist and Marxist-Leninist regimes did previously, Islamic fundamentalist regimes that become increasingly embattled domestically may abandon their zeal for exporting revolution in return for help from the status quo powers to remain in office. It would be highly ironic if, as much as they oppose them now, the major status quo powers at some point in the future provided substantial military assistance to nondemocratic but derevolutionized Islamic fundamentalist regimes fighting against their internal opponents, who may be aspiring revolutionaries belonging to yet another expanding nondemocratic revolutionary wave.

Epilogue

OTHER NONDEMOCRATIC REVOLUTIONARY WAVES

Will other nondemocratic revolutionary waves that expand via affiliate revolution arise? It is only possible to address this question in terms of possibilities, not probabilities. A basic requirement for such a revolutionary wave to emerge is the existence of a revolutionary ideology that appeals to important audiences in many countries. Both Samuel Huntington and Graham Fuller have predicted that, instead of leading to the triumph of liberal democracy throughout the world, the collapse of Marxism-Leninism will lead to the rise of other anti-Western, antidemocratic ideologies to challenge it (Huntington 1993; Fuller 1995). But not all anti-Western, antidemocratic ideologies can serve as the basis of a nondemocratic revolutionary wave.

Narrow nationalism may appeal to important audiences in one country, in a portion of one country, or in one country and limited areas in neighboring ones. Narrow nationalism may also form the basis of a nondemocratic revolutionary wave that spreads primarily via invasion. But narrow nationalism cannot inspire affiliate revolution outside of its ethnic base. Russian nationalism, for example, may or may not appeal to Russians, but it certainly has no appeal among non-Russians.

To inspire affiliate revolutions, a revolutionary ideology must have transnational appeal. What other revolutionary ideologies, or even bases for such ideologies, exist that could have a wide enough appeal to inspire affiliate revolutions in more than one country?

Mark Juergensmeyer has pointed out that religion can serve as the basis for a revolutionary ideology. His book, *The New Cold War?* discusses the emergence not only of nondemocratic Islamic revolutionaries, but also Jewish, Hindu, Sikh, Buddhist, and Christian ones (1993, passim). But while these other religions may give rise to revolutionary movements, not all religions have the same potential for giving rise to international revolutionary waves. While it is possible that religious revolutionary movements, just like religions themselves, may win converts from other religions, their most likely proponents are those who already adhere to the religious tradition from which the revolutionary movement stems. And not all religions have as broad or deep an international following as others.

Thus, Hindu fundamentalism, which Juergensmeyer describes as gaining strength, is highly unlikely to form the basis of an international revolutionary wave since there are no predominantly Hindu countries to which it could spread outside India except relatively small ones, such as Nepal and part of Sri Lanka. While Jewish and Sikh communities exist in many countries, they are minorities everywhere except Israel and the Punjab. Revolutionary movements based on these religions cannot—and, in fact, do not aim to—inspire international revolutionary movements in the sense of attempting to seize power in several countries, but focus their efforts instead on either the maintenance or creation of a single "homeland."

In order for a religion to form the basis of a revolutionary wave capable of expanding via affiliate revolutions the way Islamic fundamentalism has (and has further potential to do), its adherents must form a large proportion of the population (if not always the majority) in several countries. There are very few other religions besides Islam that meet this criterion. Buddhism could conceivably form the basis of a nondemocratic revolutionary wave that might gain a wide following in Sri Lanka (where such a movement already exists among the majority Sinhalese), Thailand, Indochina, Burma, and Tibet. Confucian fundamentalism might serve to replace increasingly discredited Marxism-Leninism in China, to justify continued nondemocratic rule in that country, and (unlike Marxism-Leninism) to serve as the basis for uniting China with the "Overseas Chinese" in Taiwan, Singapore, Malaysia, and elsewhere. Finally, "liberation theology"—a mixture of Catholicism and Marxism—may yet inspire a revolutionary wave with the potential for spreading revolution through Latin America.

It may be argued that some of these religions are not likely to spawn anything more than anemic revolutionary movements at most since fomenting revolution would represent a complete break with their tradition of passive acquiescence to existing secular authority or even support for it.

Throughout much of its history, though, Islam has also been unrevolutionary, yet revolutionary variants of it have emerged and grown powerful (Keddie 1994). The development of revolutionary strains in some other hitherto unrevolutionary religions is also occurring, and may yet develop in still others. Further, even in religions where the clergy is unrevolutionary, powerful religious revolutionary movements led by laymen can rise up, as the example of Sunni Islamic fundamentalism has shown.

There are also various pannationalisms which, like Arab nationalism attempted, could seek to unite a number of smaller nations sharing the same or similar languages, cultures, or other common features into one large nation or alliance of nations. Such pannationalist ideologies might include pan-Turanianism (attempting to unite Turkey, Azerbaijan, and the Turkic speaking peoples in Central Asia, parts of the Russian Federation, and Xinjiang), pan-Slavism (attempting to unite, or reunite, the various eastern Slavic nations—Russia, Ukraine, and Belarus—and perhaps even some of the western ones), and pannative Americanism (which could prove an especially strong force in Latin American countries where native Americans form the majority, such as Ecuador, Peru, Bolivia, and Paraguay). Particularly strong revolutionary ideologies might be created through the combination of religious and pannational elements, such as Islamic fundamentalism and pan-Turanianism, Orthodox Christian fundamentalism and pan-Slavism, Confucian fundamentalism and Chinese nationalism, or liberation theology and pannative Americanism.

Although his thesis on the inevitability that liberal democracy will triumph throughout the world has been criticized, Francis Fukuyama was right in pointing out that the collapse of Marxism-Leninism has left no other nondemocratic revolutionary ideology to challenge it on a global basis—only ones, like nationalism and religious fundamentalism, that do so on a regional or national basis (1989). Of course, another nondemocratic revolutionary ideology with global pretensions could arise or some variant of Marxism-Leninism could even be revived. There is no indication, however, that either of these developments is occurring, and they seem far less likely to emerge than regionally based religious and pannationalist ideologies.

While various forms of religious fundamentalism and pannationalism appear to be gaining strength in many countries, these ideologies face many obstacles to becoming political forces capable of launching an international revolutionary wave. And in fact they may not even attempt to do so, but may only seek to inspire religious or cultural revival movements instead.

Even if the proponents of such an ideology do attempt to launch a revolutionary wave, it may be one that collapses before achieving its grander ambitions (as occurred with pan-Africanism). However, the emergence of the Marxist-Leninist, Arab nationalist, and Islamic fundamentalist revolutionary waves as a result of the successful Russian, Egyptian, and Iranian Revolutions was not expected either. Nikki Keddie has pointed out that large events like revolutions are, by their very nature, difficult to predict (1992). So too are even larger ones such as revolutionary waves, for here two predictions are involved: 1) that a revolution espousing an internationalist revolutionary ideology will succeed somewhere; and 2) that it will further succeed in inspiring people in other countries to emulate and affiliate with it.

But while it is impossible to predict with any certainty whether any more nondemocratic revolutionary waves will arise, much less which ones, those that do are likely to be subject to the same forces preventing close lasting affiliation within a wave that afflicted previous waves: tension between neighboring states, lack of dependence on the central revolution leading to other revolutionary regimes drifting away from it, and rivalry for leadership of the wave.

Such problems are not difficult to envision within each of the potential revolutionary waves mentioned here. A Buddhist fundamentalist wave containing both Vietnam and Thailand could see the continuation of the historic rivalry between these two nations over Laos and Cambodia, the two weak nations between them. The Central Asian states would probably resist a Turkish effort to play the central revolutionary role within a pan-Turanian wave, as would the smaller states of Central Asia resist an attempt by Uzbekistan—the most populous and powerful of them—to play this role. While no other state besides Russia could play the central revolutionary role within a pan-Slavic revolutionary wave, Ukraine would probably resist its leadership, as would the western Slavic states. Similarly, just as Taiwan, Singapore, and the Overseas Chinese generally have feared domination by a Marxist-Leninist China, so too might they fear domination by a Confucian fundamentalist one. Finally, it is doubtful that common adherence to a liberation theologist and/or pannative Americanist revolutionary wave could overcome the many border disputes and rivalries that affect Latin America; it may even exacerbate them.

Just as with Marxism-Leninism, Arab nationalism, and, it is increasingly apparent, Islamic fundamentalism, other nondemocratic revolutionary waves might attempt to unite a number of different nations into a larger and more powerful whole, but narrower national, ethnic, religious, and leadership differences will work to undermine this effort. Indeed, the likelihood of conflict within some of these potential waves is so great that they might not be able to expand very far, or they may never arise at all.

AFTER THE COLLAPSE OF REVOLUTIONARY WAVES

The thrust of the argument presented here has been that nondemocratic revolutionary "for" waves that expand via affiliate revolutions eventually collapse. Others may dispute this. But whether or not the collapse of such waves is inevitable, what happens when it actually occurs? Any attempt to answer this question must necessarily be tentative since there has been even less experience with such revolutionary waves after their collapse than during them. The Arab nationalist and the Marxist-Leninist ones are the only such revolutionary waves that have collapsed so far. Further, the collapse of the Marxist-Leninist wave occurred so recently that the final nature of many of the successor regimes in several of its constituent countries (including most of the former Soviet republics) is still unsettled and evolving. Nevertheless, some patterns have emerged that point to different paths that can be taken by post–wave collapse revolutionary regimes.

The collapse of a revolutionary wave does not necessarily lead to the collapse of the regimes composing it. One path that post–wave collapse regimes have taken is to remain in power as dictatorships, sometimes with little change in the formal ideology of the regime, as did most of the post–wave collapse Arab nationalist states (Egypt, Syria, Iraq, Libya, and Algeria) and some of the Marxist-Leninist ones (China, North Korea, Vietnam, Laos, and Cuba).

Revolutionary regimes, though, can also be replaced. But the type of regime that replaces them can vary. The Marxist-Leninist case has shown that revolutionary regimes can be transformed into democracies, as appears to have occurred in most of Eastern Europe and the Baltic states and (somewhat less so) in some of the other former Soviet republics and former Marxist-Leninist regimes in the Third World. Revolutionary regimes from a collapsed nondemocratic revolutionary wave can also be replaced by revolutionary regimes from an expanding nondemocratic wave, as occurred in Sudan and Afghanistan, and threatens to occur with varying degrees of immediacy in Algeria, Egypt, Tajikistan, and perhaps elsewhere. Finally, post–wave collapse revolutionary regimes might be transformed into or replaced by nondemocratic, or partially democratic, nationalist regimes, as has already occurred or threatens to occur in many of the former Soviet republics (including Russia, Belarus, Georgia, Armenia, and Azerbaijan) as well as in Serbia and Croatia.

The reasons that some post–wave collapse revolutionary states democratize while others retain or acquire some form of dictatorship is a subject too large to address here. The choice facing such states, however, is often not a simple one between dictatorship and democracy. In chapter 2, I argued that part of the appeal of an internationalist ideology to aspiring revolutionaries and revolutionary regimes was that it justified keeping a country intact despite its internal divisions and arbitrarily drawn boundaries. But instead of genuinely uniting diverse groups within a nation as Marxism-Leninism, Arab nationalism, and Islamic fundamentalism all claimed would happen or was actually happening, these regimes often exacerbated existing differences or even created new ones. Minority groups were largely excluded from power in many countries, such as the USSR, while in others, such as Syria and Iraq, minority groups exercised power over the majority.

In many cases, there exist regionally dominant minorities—groups that are a minority in a country as whole but that are the majority in a specific region. Efforts at democratization in such countries are often accompanied by demands for secession on the part of these regionally dominant minorities. The collapse of the Marxist-Leninist revolutionary wave led not only to the rise of secessionist demands, but to their rapid achievement in an extraordinary number of countries, including the former USSR (from which the fourteen non-Russian "union republics" gained independence), former Yugoslavia (from which Slovenia, Croatia, Bosnia, and Macedonia seceded), former Czechoslovakia (which split into the Czech and Slovak Republics), and Ethiopia (which granted independence to Eritrea). Though unrecognized internationally, de facto secessions have also occurred in Russia (Chechnya), Moldova (the "Transdniester Republic"), Georgia (Abkhazia), and the Serbian-held regions of Croatia and Bosnia. In addition, a number of secessionist movements have arisen or been revived elsewhere in the former USSR, including Russia (the North Caucasus), and Georgia (South Ossetia), as well as in China (Xinjiang and Tibet). The collapse of the Marxist-Leninist wave also led to national reunification in two cases—Germany and Yemen—and it appears likely that Korea will eventually follow.

No recognized secession has occurred in any of the countries belonging to the Arab nationalist wave, but a de facto Kurdish secession has occurred in Iraq, and an attempt to reestablish South Yemeni independence after only four years of unity with North Yemen was ended by force. The policies of the post–wave collapse Arab nationalist regime in Egypt have led to the rise of an opposition movement in southern Egypt, but this has not yet developed a specifically secessionist agenda.

Nor has secession occurred in any of the few countries belonging to the Islamic fundamentalist wave, but in Iran, a movement appears to be gaining strength within "southern Azerbaijan" to unite with independent (northern) Azerbaijan (Nissman 1995). The Islamic fundamentalist regime in Sudan has been unable to defeat rebel opposition movements in the predominantly non-Muslim south.[1] The ongoing civil war among the Arabs of Algeria appears to be contributing to an increase in Berber separatism there.[2] In addition, the ongoing struggles between Islamic forces in Afghanistan reflect ethnic as well as other cleavages in that country (Dorronsoro 1995; Barfield 1996).

Post–wave collapse revolutionary states are by no means the only countries subject to secessionist movements or ethnic conflict. But to the extent that a regime change occurs or is possible in them, the tradeoffs concerning the country's future can present themselves more starkly where there are regionally dominant minorities. Although the internationalist ideology of the collapsed wave may once have convinced key elements within such minorities to support the revolution in the hope that it would lead to true equality and a share of power, disillusionment with this ideology may convince them that cooperation with the majority is impossible and that their interests can only be preserved through the creation of their own state. In such situations, the majority (or its leaders) in the rest of the country must decide which it values more: democracy or the preservation of unity. The former runs the risk that the regionally dominant minority will vote to secede. The latter runs the risk of a costly, protracted conflict to preserve unity by force.

It is not inevitable that post–wave collapse revolutionary states face these tradeoffs. States without regionally dominant minorities obviously do not, and even those with regionally dominant minorities may succeed in both building democracy and preserving unity peacefully. But this clearly has not happened in those states of the collapsed Marxist-Leninist wave in which secession has already occurred. Indeed, the success of secession in so many countries in so short a period has probably bolstered those forces seeking it in other post–wave collapse Marxist-Leninist and Arab nationalist states, in Islamic fundamentalist regimes, and in other countries. The most enduring legacy of these three nondemocratic "for" waves that expand via affiliate revolution may be that they triggered a mighty secessionist "against" wave that seeks to fragment multiethnic states.

Notes

Chapter 1

1. Useful summaries and critiques of the literature on the causes of revolution can be found in Goldstone (1980), Knutsen and Bailey (1989), and Sederberg (1994, 113-200).

2. Barrington Moore observed that, "By themselves the peasants have never been able to accomplish a revolution. . . . The peasants have to have leaders from other classes" (1966, 479). He further noted that even when peasant revolution succeeds, the peasants have been "its first victims" (1966, 480).

3. "C.I.A. Spent Millions to Support Japanese Right in 50's and 60's," *The New York Times,* 9 October 1994.

4. "Turn Back, Mubarak," *The Economist,* 4 February 1995, 15.

5. In *The Third Wave: Democratization in the Late Twentieth Century* (1991), Huntington argues that democratization has occurred in three distinct waves. After each of the first two, however, there was a "reverse wave," in which several democracies reverted to authoritarianism. Thus, after this third, most recent democratic wave (encompassing the collapse of communism), a third reverse wave can be expected. But Huntington also notes that the first two reverse waves involved fewer conversions from democracy to dictatorship than conversions from dictatorship to democracy in the democratic waves they followed. Further, Huntington argues that the states that experienced some period of interrupted democratization in the past have made more durable transitions from dictatorship to democracy in the third wave than those that have never experienced democratization. Some new third-wave democracies, then, may well be replaced by authoritarian regimes in a third reverse wave, but those that do are likely to be candidates for a more durable democratic transition in a fourth wave.

Huntington notes that there are no civilizational or cultural barriers to democracy. To those who say that Islam is incompatible with democracy, Huntington responds that people used to make the same argument about Catholicism (310-11). While Huntington does not predict the universal spread of democracy, he does present a model in which it spreads further and further indefinitely, even after reverse waves are taken into account.

6. According to Samuel Huntington, American support was "critical" to democratic transitions in ten countries and a "contributing factor" in six others during the "third wave." He concluded that "the absence of the United States from the process would have meant fewer and later transitions to democracy" (1991, 98).

Philippe Schmitter, by contrast, argued that "it was the *decline* not the rise in U.S. power that seemed to open up spaces for political change. . . . it was precisely in those countries where the influence of the United States remained the greatest, the Caribbean and Central America, where the progress toward democracy was the least advanced" (1995, 507).

Chapter 2

1. The revolutionary leaders of Russia, Egypt, and Iran, however, were not the first to expound their revolutionary ideology, at least in general terms. Marxism had been intellectually popular for several decades in Western Europe, where several Marxist political parties had sprung up and achieved a far greater degree of political importance in their countries than had the Bolsheviks even a few months before seizing power in Russia (Kolakowski 1978).

Arab nationalism had also been present in the Middle East long before the rise of 'Abd al-Nasir. The Hashemite monarchies, which the British installed in Iraq and Jordan after World War I, espoused an anti-Ottoman but pro-Western form of Arab nationalism. But as Hanna Batatu wrote with regard to the Iraqi king, "By deferring to the English, Faisal alienated popular opinion" (1978, 326). In addition, Michel 'Aflaq and the Ba'th party, which was first organized in Syria, advocated an anti-Western, revolutionary Arab nationalism for over a decade before 'Abd al-Nasir came to power in Egypt (Batatu 1978, 722-48).

Furthermore, there were efforts to create a pan-Islamic political movement long before the rise of the Ayatollah Khomeini (Landau 1994). The spread of Saudi power in the 1920s from Najd, in the center of the Arabian Peninsula, to all of what is now Saudi Arabia, was the result of an anti-British Islamic fundamentalist revolutionary movement (the Ikhwan), which King 'Abd al-'Aziz led but then crushed in 1929-30 when it threatened to escape from his control (Holden and Johns 1981, 69-93). As its cooperation with and dependence on the West increased afterward, the Saudi monarchy lost whatever revolutionary credentials it may have had.

2. According to Colburn, many of those who became the leaders of Third World Marxist-Leninist movements learned their Marxism-Leninism at North American or West European universities, and had never even visited the USSR before they came to power (1994, 20-35). There is much anecdotal evidence to suggest that a considerable proportion of those students who did pursue higher education in the USSR or Eastern Europe became disillusioned with Marxism-Leninism as a result.

3. Shi'ite opposition to Bahrain's ruling family (which belongs to the Sunni minority on the island) arose again in 1994-95, but Iran does not appear to be involved in this movement (John Lancaster, "The Two Worlds of Bahrain," *Washington Post,* 13 June 1995).

    The Saudi government has claimed that the June 1996 truck bombing of an American military housing complex in Dhahran was "backed" by Iran. Several U.S. government officials, however, saw the Saudi claim as being "colored by a desire to assign some of the blame for the embarrassing blast to Iran . . . rather than to domestic Saudi dissidents" (R. Jeffrey Smith, "Saudis Hold Forty Suspects in GI Quarters Bombing," *Washington Post,* 1 November 1996).

4. John F. Burns, "Afghanistan Reels Back into View," *The New York Times,* 6 October 1996.

5. See also Robin Wright, "Iran Extends Reach of Its Aid to Islamic Groups, *Los Angeles Times,* 6 April 1993.

6. Chris Hedges, "Sudan Linked to Rebellion in Algeria," *The New York Times,* 24 December 1994.

7. "Defeat of Kabul Leaders Scuttles Pact with Moscow," Jamestown Foundation *Monitor,* 1 October 1996.

8. For surveys on Russian public opinion regarding the war in Tajikistan, see U.S. Information Agency Office of Research and Media Reaction, "Russians Desire Cooperation with the West, Are Wary of Entanglements in the 'Near Abroad,'" *Opinion Research Memorandum* M-176-94, 3 August 1994; and *idem.,* "Environment and Nuclear Proliferation Are Among Russians' Top Concerns," *Russia/NIS Opinion Alert* L-68-95, 13 November 1995. See also "Hold Your Breath," *The Economist,* 15 March 1997, 39-40.

9. Michael Field, "How to Stop Militant Islam," *The New York Times,* 3 July 1995.

10. Sally Ann Baynard, "Fundamentalist Error," *Washington Post,* 29 August 1994.

11. Amos Perlmutter, "Wishful Thinking About Islamic Fundamentalism," *Washington Post,* 19 January 1992; Daniel Pipes, "Algerian Time Bomb," *Washington Post,* 11 August 1994.

Chapter 3

1. "Last Throw," *The Economist,* 2 November 1996, 35.

2. See also "Defeat of Kabul Leaders Scuttles Pact with Moscow," Jamestown Foundation *Monitor,* 1 October 1996.

3. As this was being written, the Taliban—which seized Kabul in September 1996—had not yet met this test.

4. "News and Comments," *Central Asia Monitor,* no. 4, 1995, 5.

Chapter 4

1. Vyacheslav Dashichev, "East-West: Quest for New Relations: On the Priorities of the Soviet State's Foreign Policy," *Literaturnaia Gazeta,* 18 May 1988 in FBIS-SOV-88-098, 20 May 1988, 4-8.

2. *Africa South of the Sahara* 1994, 135-36; "Trying," *The Economist,* 15 July 1995, 28-29. The MPLA and UNITA, however, still control separate sections of the country, and the peace between them is tenuous; "Still Waiting for Peace," *The Economist,* 29 March 1997, 48.

3. Larry Rohter, "Critics Question Nicaraguan Army's Makeover," *The New York Times,* 16 July 1995.

4. "Democracy 2, Sandinists 0," *The Economist,* 26 October 1996, 50.

5. Michael Dobbs, "Vietnam, U.S. Begin a New Relationship," *Washington Post,* 6 August 1995.

6. Gillian Gunn, "Over Troubled Waters," *Washington Post,* 21 May 1995.

7. "Economic Strains Test Iran's Islamic Government," *Washington Post,* 5 October 1994.

8. *Ibid.*

9. "Discontent Grows in Iranian Cities," *The New York Times,* 14 August 1991; "Inflation Fuels Discontent Against Iran's Government," *The New York Times,* 20 November 1994; "Iranian City Calm After Clashes," *Washington Post,* 8 December 1996.

10. "Don't Count on Us, Ayatollah," *The Economist,* 27 August 1994, 34; Nora Boustany, "Iran's Army Refused to Intervene in City's Anti-Government Riot," *Washington Post,* 7 October 1994.

11. Robin Wright, "Islamist's Theory of Relativity," *Los Angeles Times,* 27 January 1995.

12. Tehran's enmity for the Taliban is so great that shortly after the latter seized Kabul, "Iran denounced the Taliban as stooges of Pakistan and therefore, by Iran's reasoning, of the United States, and signaled that it would not acquiesce in Taliban rule over the entire country" (Thomas W. Lippman, "State Dept. Sees Little Hope for Quick End to Afghan Civil War," *Washington Post,* 4 November 1994).

13. Robin Wright, "Mullah Maneuvers into Power," *Los Angeles Times,* 6 June 1995.

14. "[I]f property was a divine gift, as Khomeini argued, then the government, as long as it was God's government, had the ultimate right to defend and oversee private property. If mankind was inherently evil, irrational, and violent, then individual liberty was an open invitation to social chaos. Democracy paved the way to anarchy. Unbridled pluralism invited internal disorder. If individuals were instinctively rapacious, then strong authority was needed to preserve private property" (Abrahamian 1993, 44).

Chapter 5

1. David B. Ottaway, "Wielding Aid, U.S. Targets Sudan," *Washington Post,* 10 November 1996.

2. The Taliban, who reportedly did receive external assistance from Pakistan, appear to be an exception to this rule. In this case, however, the ouster of the Rabbani government from Kabul in 1996 did not lead to the withdrawal of Afghanistan from the Islamic fundamentalist revolutionary wave, since the Taliban are also—indeed, far more extreme—Islamic fundamentalist revolutionaries.

3. Andrew Rosenthal, "Where Do Interests of U.S. Lie: In United or Divided USSR?" *The New York Times,* 28 July 1991; Francis X. Clines, "Bush, in

Ukraine, Walks Fine Line on Sovereignty," *The New York Times,* 2 August 1991; Andrew Rosenthal, "In Bush's Councils, a Growing Distrust of Yeltsin," *The New York Times,* 2 September 1991.

Epilogue

1. Jonathan C. Randal, "Sudanese Civil War Proves Resilient," *Washington Post,* 6 May 1995.

2. "Man Alive," *The Economist,* 15 October 1994.

Bibliography

Abrahamian, Ervand. 1993. *Khomeinism: Essays on the Islamic Republic.* Berkeley: University of California Press.

Africa South of the Sahara 1994. 1994. London: Europa Publications.

Ahmad, Eqbal. 1982. "Comments on Skocpol." *Theory and Society.* 11 (May): 293-300.

Ajami, Fouad. 1992. *The Arab Predicament: Arab Political Thought and Practice since 1967.* Updated ed. Cambridge: Cambridge University Press.

Akehurst, John. 1982. *We Won a War: The Campaign in Oman, 1965-1975.* Wilton, UK: Michael Russell.

Arjomand, Said Amir. 1991. "A Victory for the Pragmatists: The Islamic Fundamentalist Reaction in Iran." In *Islamic Fundamentalisms and the Gulf Crisis,* edited by James Piscatori. Chicago: American Academy of Arts and Sciences.

Armstrong, David. 1993. *Revolution and World Order: The Revolutionary State in International Society.* Oxford: Oxford University Press.

Aslund, Anders. 1989. *Gorbachev's Struggle for Economic Reform: The Soviet Reform Process, 1985-88.* Ithaca, NY: Cornell University Press.

Auda, Gehad. 1991. "An Uncertain Response: The Islamic Movement in Egypt." In *Islamic Fundamentalisms and the Gulf Crisis,* edited by James Piscatori. Chicago: American Academy of Arts and Sciences.

Ayubi, Nazih N. 1991. *Political Islam: Religion and Politics in the Arab World.* London: Routledge.

Bach, Quintin V. S. 1987. *Soviet Economic Assistance to the Less Developed Countries: A Statistical Analysis.* Oxford: Oxford University Press.

Bakhash, Shaul. 1984. *The Reign of the Ayatollahs: Iran and the Islamic Revolution.* New York: Basic Books.

Barfield, Thomas. 1996. "The Afghan Morass." *Current History.* 95 (January): 38-43.

Batatu, Hanna. 1978. *The Old Social Classes and the Revolutionary Movements of Iraq: A Study of Iraq's Old Landed and Commercial Classes and of its Communists, Ba'thists, and Free Officers.* Princeton: Princeton University Press.

————. 1983. *The Egyptian, Syrian, and Iraqi Revolutions: Some Observations on Their Underlying Causes and Social Character.* Washington, DC: Georgetown University Center for Contemporary Arab Studies.

Biberaj, Elez. 1985. "Albania after Hoxha: Dilemmas of Change." *Problems of Communism.* 34 (November-December): 32-47.

Binder, Leonard. 1988. *Islamic Liberalism: A Critique of Development Ideologies.* Chicago: University of Chicago Press.

Bishku, Michael. 1991. "Iraq's Claim to Kuwait: A Historical Overview." *American-Arab Affairs.* No. 37 (Summer): 77-88.

Blasier, Cole. 1991. "Moscow's Retreat from Cuba." *Problems of Communism.* 40 (November-December): 91-99.

Bowen, Merle L. 1990. "Economic Crisis in Mozambique." *Current History.* 89 (May): 217-20, 226-28.

Bradsher, Henry S. 1985. *Afghanistan and the Soviet Union.* Rev. ed. Durham, NC: Duke University Press.

Brinton, Crane. 1965. *The Anatomy of Revolution.* 3rd ed. New York: Vintage Books.

Brzezinski, Zbigniew. 1983. *Power and Principle: Memoirs of the National Security Adviser, 1977-1981.* New York: Farrar Straus Giroux.

Cassandra [pseud]. 1995. "The Impending Crisis in Egypt." *The Middle East Journal.* 49 (Winter): 9-27.

Chubin, Shahram. 1994. "Iran's Military Intentions and Capabilities." In *Iran's Strategic Intentions and Capabilities,* edited by Patrick Clawson. Washington, DC: National Defense University.

Cigar, Norman. 1989. "Soviet-South Yemeni Relations: The Gorbachev Years." *Journal of South Asian and Middle Eastern Studies.* 12 (Summer): 3-38.

Clawson, Patrick. 1994. "Alternative Foreign Policy Views Among the Iranian Policy Elite." In *Iran's Strategic Intentions and Capabilities,* edited by Patrick Clawson. Washington, DC: National Defense University.

Colburn, Forrest D. 1994. *The Vogue of Revolution in Poor Countries.* Princeton, NJ: Princeton University Press.

Cordesman, Anthony H. 1994. *Iran and Iraq: The Threat from the Northern Gulf.* Boulder, CO: Westview Press.

Dawisha, Adeed. 1986. *The Arab Radicals.* New York: Council on Foreign Relations.

Dawisha, Karen. 1990. *Eastern Europe, Gorbachev, and Reform: The Great Challenge,* 2d ed. Cambridge: Cambridge University Press.

Deeb, Mary-Jane. 1989. "Inter-Maghribi Relations since 1969: A Study of the Modalities of Unions and Mergers." *The Middle East Journal.* 43 (Winter): 20-33.

Dommen, Arthur J. 1995. "Laos in 1994: Among Generals, Among Friends." *Asian Survey.* 35 (January): 84-91.

Dorronsoro, Gilles. 1995. "Afghanistan's Civil War." *Current History.* 94 (January): 37-40.

Dunbar, Charles. 1992. "The Unification of Yemen: Process, Politics, and Prospects." *The Middle East Journal.* 46 (Summer): 456-76.

Duncanson, Dennis. 1981. "Lessons of Modern History: The British Experience." In *U.S. Policy and Low-Intensity Conflict,* edited by Sam C. Sarkesian and William L. Scully. New Brunswick, NJ: Transaction Books.

Entelis, John P. 1995. "Political Islam in Algeria: The Nonviolent Dimension." *Current History.* 94 (January): 13-17.

Esposito, John L. 1992. *The Islamic Threat: Myth or Reality?* New York: Oxford University Press.

Fandy, Mamoun. 1994. "Egypt's Islamic Group: Regional Revenge?" *The Middle East Journal.* 48 (Autumn): 607-25.

Farhi, Farideh. 1990. *States and Urban-Based Revolutions: Iran and Nicaragua.* Urbana, IL: University of Illinois Press.

Farid, Abdel Magid. 1994. *Nasser: The Final Years.* Reading, UK: Ithaca Press.

Finnegan, William. 1992. *A Complicated War: The Harrowing of Mozambique.* Berkeley: University of California Press.

Fukuyama, Francis. 1985. "The Rise and Fall of the Marxist-Leninist Vanguard Party." *Survey.* 29 (Summer): 116-35.

———. 1989. "The End of History?" *The National Interest.* No. 16 (Summer): 3-18.

Fuller, Graham. 1991. *The "Center of the Universe": The Geopolitics of Iran.* Boulder, CO: Westview Press.

———. 1995. "The Next Ideology." *Foreign Policy.* No. 98 (Spring): 145-58.

Garcia, Jose Z. 1990. "Tragedy in El Salvador." *Current History.* 89 (January): 9-12, 40-41.

Garthoff, Raymond L. 1985. *Detente and Confrontation: American-Soviet Relations from Nixon to Reagan.* Washington, DC: The Brookings Institution.

Gause, F. Gregory, III. 1990. *Saudi-Yemeni Relations: Domestic Structures and Foreign Influence.* New York: Columbia University Press.

Golan, Galia. 1988. *The Soviet Union and National Liberation Movements in the Third World.* Boston: Unwin Hyman.

Goldstone, Jack A. 1980. "Theories of Revolution: The Third Generation." *World Politics.* 32 (April): 425-53.

Goodman, Allan E. 1995. "Vietnam in 1994: With Peace at Hand." *Asian Survey.* 35 (January): 92-99.

Goodwin, Jeff, and Theda Skocpol. 1989. "Explaining Revolutions in the Contemporary Third World." *Politics & Society.* 17 (December): 489-509.

Greenfeld, Liah. 1992. *Nationalism: Five Roads to Modernity.* Cambridge, MA: Harvard University Press.

Gwertzman, Bernard, and Michael T. Kaufman, eds. 1990. *The Collapse of Communism,* rev. ed. New York: Times Books/Random House.

Haddad, Yvonne. 1992. "Islamists and the 'Problem of Israel.'" *The Middle East Journal.* 46 (Spring): 266-85.

Halliday, Fred. 1974. *Arabia without Sultans.* Harmondsworth, UK: Penguin Books.

————. 1994. "An Elusive Normalization: Western Europe and the Iranian Revolution." *The Middle East Journal.* 48 (Spring): 309-26.

Halperin, Morton H., and David J. Scheffer with Patricia L. Small. 1992. *Self-Determination in the New World Order.* Washington, DC: Carnegie Endowment for International Peace.

Holden, David, and Richard Johns. 1981. *The House of Saud: The Rise and Rule of the Most Powerful Dynasty in the Arab World.* New York: Holt, Rinehart and Winston.

Holtman, Robert B. 1967. *The Napoleonic Revolution.* Philadelphia: J. B. Lippincott.

Hooglund, Eric. 1990. "Strategic and Political Objectives in the Gulf War." In *The Persian Gulf War: Lessons for Strategy, Law, and Diplomacy,* edited by Christopher C. Joyner. New York: Greenwood Press.

Horne, Alistair. 1977. *A Savage War of Peace: Algeria, 1954-1962.* New York: Viking Press.

Hourani, Albert. 1991. *A History of the Arab Peoples.* Cambridge, MA: Harvard University Press.

Hudson, Michael C. 1995. "Bipolarity, Rational Calculation, and War in Yemen." In *The Yemeni War of 1994: Causes and Consequences,* edited by Jamal S. al-Suwaidi. London: Saqi Books.

Hume, Cameron. 1994. *Ending Mozambique's War: the Role of Mediation and Good Offices.* Washington, DC: United States Institute of Peace Press.

Huntington, Samuel P. 1991. *The Third Wave: Democratization in the Late Twentieth Century.* Norman: University of Oklahoma Press.

————. 1993. "The Clash of Civilizations?" *Foreign Affairs.* 72 (Summer): 22-49.

Hutchcroft, Paul D. 1995. "Unraveling the Past in the Philippines." *Current History.* 94 (December): 430-34.

Jelavich, Barbara. 1983. *History of the Balkans,* vol. 2, *Twentieth Century.* Cambridge: Cambridge University Press.

Johnson, A. Ross. 1984. "The Warsaw Pact: Soviet Military Policy in Eastern Europe." In *Soviet Policy in Eastern Europe,* edited by Sarah Meiklejohn Terry. New Haven: Yale University Press.

Juergensmeyer, Mark. 1993. *The New Cold War? Religious Nationalism Confronts the Secular State.* Berkeley: University of California Press.

Karshenas, Massoud, and M. Hashem Pesaran. 1995. "Economic Reform and the Reconstruction of the Iranian Economy." *The Middle East Journal.* 49 (Winter): 89-111.

Katz, Mark N. 1982. *The Third World in Soviet Military Thought.* Baltimore: Johns Hopkins University Press.

———. 1983. "The Soviet-Cuban Connection." *International Security.* 8 (Summer): 88-112.

———. 1986. *Russia and Arabia: Soviet Foreign Policy toward the Arabian Peninsula.* Baltimore: Johns Hopkins University Press.

———. 1987. "Anti-Soviet Insurgencies: Growing Trend or Passing Phase?" In *The Soviet Union, Eastern Europe and the Third World,* edited by Roger E. Kanet. Cambridge: Cambridge University Press.

———. 1988-89. "Camels and Commissars." *The National Interest.* No. 14 (Winter): 121-24.

———. 1989. "Evolving Soviet Perceptions of U.S. Strategy." *The Washington Quarterly.* 12 (Summer): 157-67.

———. 1990a. "Why Does the Cold War Continue in the Third World?" *Journal of Peace Research.* 27 (November): 353-57.

———. 1990b. "Gorbachev and Revolution." In *The USSR and Marxist Revolutions in the Third World,* edited by Mark N. Katz. Cambridge: Cambridge University Press.

———. 1995a. "Emerging Patterns in the International Relations of Central Asia." In *The Making of Foreign Policy in Russia and the New States of Eurasia,* edited by Adeed Dawisha and Karen Dawisha. Armonk, NY: M.E. Sharpe.

————. 1995b. "External Powers and the Yemeni Civil War." In *The Yemeni War of 1994: Causes and Consequences,* edited by Jamal S. al-Suwaidi. London: Saqi Books.

————. 1995-96. "An Emerging Russian-Iranian Alliance?" *Caspian Crossroads.* No. 4 (Winter): 21-24.

Katzman, Kenneth. 1993. *The Warriors of Islam: Iran's Revolutionary Guard.* Boulder, CO: Westview Press.

————. 1994. Iran and the Export of the Islamic Revolution. Lecture presented at the Washington Institute for Near East Policy, 29 November.

Keddie, Nikki R. 1992. "Can Revolutions Be Predicted; Can Their Causes Be Understood?" *Contention.* 1 (Winter): 159-82.

————. 1994. "The Revolt of Islam, 1700 to 1993: Comparative Considerations and Relations to Imperialism." *Comparative Studies in Society and History.* 36 (July): 463-87.

Kerr, Malcom H. 1971. *The Arab Cold War.* London: Royal Institute of International Affairs/Oxford University Press.

al-Khalil, Samir. 1989. *Republic of Fear: The Politics of Modern Iraq.* Berkeley: University of California Press.

Kirkpatrick, Jeane. 1979. "Dictatorships and Double Standards." *Commentary.* 68 (November): 34-45.

Knutsen, Torbjorn L. 1992. "The Reagan Doctrine and the Lessons from the Afghan War." *Australian Journal of Politics and History.* 38, no. 2: 193-205.

Knutsen, Torbjorn L., and Jennifer L. Bailey. 1989. "Over the Hill? *The Anatomy of Revolution* at Fifty." *Journal of Peace Research.* 26 (November): 421-31.

Kolakowski, Leszek. 1978. *Main Currents of Marxism,* vol. 2, *The Golden Age.* Oxford: Oxford University Press.

Lamote, Laurent. 1994. "Iran's Foreign Policy and Internal Crises." In *Iran's Strategic Intentions and Capabilities,* edited by Patrick Clawson. Washington, DC: National Defense University.

Landau, Jacob M. 1994. *The Politics of Pan-Islam.* Oxford: Oxford University Press.

Lee, Manwoo. 1993. "The Two Koreas and the Unification Game." *Current History.* 92 (December): 421-25.

Legrain, Jean-Francois. 1991. "A Defining Moment: Palestinian Islamic Fundamentalism." In *Islamic Fundamentalisms and the Gulf Crisis,* edited by James Piscatori. Chicago: American Academy of Arts and Sciences.

Lenczowski, George. 1980. *The Middle East in World Affairs.* 4th ed. Ithaca, NY: Cornell University Press.

Limberg, Wayne P. 1990. "Soviet Military Support for Third-World Marxist Regimes." In *The USSR and Marxist Revolutions in the Third World,* edited by Mark N. Katz. Cambridge: Cambridge University Press.

Lloyd, Robert B. 1995. "Mozambique: The Terror of War, the Tensions of Peace." *Current History.* 94 (April): 152-55.

Low, D. A. 1991. *Eclipse of Empire.* Cambridge: Cambridge University Press.

Lynch, Allen, and Reneo Lukic. 1993. "Russian Foreign Policy and the Wars in the Former Yugoslavia." *RFE/RL Research Report.* 2 (15 October): 25-32.

MacFarlane, S. Neil. 1985. *Superpower Rivalry and Third World Radicalism: The Idea of National Liberation.* London: Croom Helm.

————. 1990. "Successes and Failures in Soviet Policy toward Marxist Revolutions in the Third World, 1917-1985." In *The USSR and Marxist Revolutions in the Third World,* edited by Mark N. Katz. Cambridge: Cambridge University Press.

————. 1992. "Soviet-Angolan Relations: 1975-1990." In *Soviet Policy in Africa: From the Old to the New Thinking,* edited by George W. Breslauer. Berkeley: Berkeley-Stanford Program in Soviet Studies and Center for Slavic and East European Studies, University of California at Berkeley.

Mawdsley, Evan. 1987. *The Russian Civil War.* Boston: Unwin Hyman.

McDaniel, Tim. 1991. *Autocracy, Modernization, and Revolution in Russia and Iran.* Princeton, NJ: Princeton University Press.

McLachlan, Keith. 1994. "Introduction." In *The Boundaries of Modern Iran,* edited by Keith McLachlan. London: UCL Press.

Mills, Richard M. 1990. *As Moscow Sees Us: American Politics and Society in the Soviet Mindset.* New York: Oxford University Press.

Moore, Barrington, Jr. 1966. *Social Origins of Dictatorship and Democracy: Lord and Peasant in the Making of the Modern World.* Boston: Beacon Press.

Munson, Henry, Jr. 1988. *Islam and Revolution in the Middle East.* New Haven: Yale University Press.

Muslih, Muhammad. 1995. "Arafat's Dilemma." *Current History.* 94 (January): 23-27.

Nahaylo, Bohdan, and Victor Swoboda. 1990. *Soviet Disunion: A History of the Nationalities Problem in the USSR.* New York: The Free Press.

Nasser, Gamal Abdul. 1955. *Egypt's Liberation: The Philosophy of the Revolution.* Washington, DC: Public Affairs Press.

Nissman, David. 1995. "A New Force in Azerbaijani-Iranian Relations." Jamestown Foundation *Prism.* 1 (12 May): 5-6.

Panico, Christopher J. 1993. "Uzbekistan's Southern Diplomacy." *RFE/RL Research Report.* 2 (26 March): 39-45.

Patman, Robert G. 1990. *The Soviet Union in the Horn of Africa: The Diplomacy of Intervention and Disengagement.* Cambridge: Cambridge University Press.

Pike, Douglas. 1987. *Vietnam and the Soviet Union: Anatomy of an Alliance.* Boulder, CO: Westview Press.

Piscatori, James P. 1986. *Islam in a World of Nation-States.* Cambridge: Cambridge University Press.

Porter, Bruce D. 1984. *The USSR in Third World Conflicts.* Cambridge: Cambridge University Press.

Post, Jerrold M. 1995. "Cuba's Maximal Leader Under Maximal Stress." *Problems of Post-Communism.* 42 (March-April): 34-38.

Pridham, Geoffrey. 1991. "The Politics of the European Community, Transnational Networks and Democratic Transition in Southern Europe." In *Encouraging Democracy: The International Context of Regime Transition in Southern Europe,* edited by Geoffrey Pridham. Leicester: Leicester University Press.

———. 1994. "The International Dimension of Democratisation: Theory, Practice, and Inter-Regional Comparisons." In *Building Democracy? The International Dimension of Democratisation in Eastern*

Europe, edited by Geoffrey Pridham, Eric Herring, and George Sanford. New York: St. Martin's Press.

Rais, Rasul Bakhsh. 1992. "Afghanistan After the Soviet Withdrawal." *Current History.* 91 (March): 123-27.

Ramazani, R. K. 1992. "Iran's Foreign Policy: Both North and South." *The Middle East Journal.* 46 (Summer): 393-412.

Remnek, Richard B. 1992. "Translating 'New Thinking' into Practice: The Case of Ethiopia." In *Soviet Policy in Africa: From the Old to the New Thinking,* edited by George W. Breslauer. Berkeley: Berkeley-Stanford Program in Soviet Studies and Center for Slavic and East European Studies, University of California at Berkeley.

Rodman, Peter W. 1994. *More Precious Than Peace: The Cold War Struggle for the Third World.* New York: Charles Scribner's Sons.

Roy, Olivier. 1994. *The Failure of Political Islam.* Translated by Carol Volk. Cambridge, MA: Harvard University Press.

Rubin, Barnett R. 1994. "Tajikistan: From Soviet Republic to Russian-Uzbek Protectorate." In *Central Asia and the World: Kazakhstan, Uzbekistan, Tajikistan, Kyrgyzstan, and Turkmenistan,* edited by Michael Mandelbaum. New York: Council on Foreign Relations Press.

Rubinstein, Alvin Z. 1988. *Moscow's Third World Strategy.* Princeton, NJ: Princeton University Press.

————. 1992. *Soviet Foreign Policy since World War II: Imperial and Global,* 4th ed. New York: Harper Collins.

Sachedina, Abdulaziz A. 1991. "Activist Shi'ism in Iran, Iraq, and Lebanon." In *The Fundamentalism Project,* vol. 1, *Fundamentalisms Observed,* edited by Martin E. Marty and R. Scott Appleby. Chicago: University of Chicago Press.

Safran, Nadav. 1969. *From War to War: The Arab-Israeli Confrontation, 1948-1967.* Indianapolis: Pegasus.

Sakwa, Richard. 1990. *Gorbachev and His Reforms, 1985-1990.* New York: Prentice Hall.

Schmitter, Philippe C. 1995. "The International Context of Contemporary Democratization." In *Transitions to Democracy: Comparative Per-*

spectives from Southern Europe, Latin America and Eastern Europe, edited by Geoffrey Pridham. Aldershot, UK: Dartmouth.

Sederberg, Peter C. 1994. *Fires Within: Political Violence and Revolutionary Change.* New York: Harper Collins.

Sick, Gary. 1986. *All Fall Down: America's Tragic Encounter with Iran.* New York: Penguin Books.

Simon, Jeffrey D. 1989. *Revolutions Without Guerrillas.* R-3683-RC. Santa Monica, CA: The RAND Corp.

Skocpol, Theda. 1979. *States and Social Revolutions: A Comparative Analysis of France, Russia, and China.* Cambridge: Cambridge University Press.

———. 1994. *Social Revolutions in the Modern World.* Cambridge: Cambridge University Press.

Smith, Tony. 1994. *America's Mission: The United States and the Worldwide Struggle for Democracy in the Twentieth Century.* Princeton, NJ: Princeton University Press.

Stookey, Robert W. 1978. *Yemen: The Politics of the Yemen Arab Republic.* Boulder, CO: Westview Press.

Strategic Survey. Annual. London: International Institute for Strategic Studies.

Tarling, Nicholas. 1966. *A Concise History of Southeast Asia.* New York: Frederick A. Praeger.

Turabi, Hasan. 1992. "Islam, Democracy, the State and the West." Lecture and discussion summarized by Louis J. Cantori and Arthur Lowrie. *Middle East Policy.* 1, no. 3: 49-73.

Ulam, Adam B. 1974. *Expansion and Coexistence: Soviet Foreign Policy, 1917-73,* 2nd ed. New York: Praeger Publishers.

———. 1983. *Dangerous Relations: The Soviet Union in World Politics, 1970-1982.* New York: Oxford University Press.

Um, Khatharya. 1995. "Cambodia in 1994: The Year of Transition." *Asian Survey.* 35 (January): 76-83.

U.S. Arms Control and Disarmament Agency. 1988. *World Military Expenditures and Arms Transfers, 1987.* Washington, DC: U.S. Government Printing Office.

Valenta, Jiri, and Virginia Valenta. 1986. "Leninism in Grenada." In *Grenada and Soviet/Cuban Policy: Internal Crisis and U.S./OECS Intervention,* edited by Jiri Valenta and Herbert J. Ellison. Boulder, CO: Westview Press.

Warburg, Gabriel R. 1990. "The *Sharia* in Sudan: Implementation and Repercussions, 1983-1989." *The Middle East Journal.* 44 (Autumn): 624-37.

Whelan, Joseph G., and Michael J. Dixon. 1986. *The Soviet Union in the Third World: Threat to World Peace?* Washington, DC: Pergamon-Brassey's.

White, Stephen. 1990. *Gorbachev in Power.* Cambridge: Cambridge University Press.

Wickham, Carrie Rosefsky. 1994. "Beyond Democratization: Political Change in the Arab World." *PS: Political Science & Politics.* 27 (September): 507-09.

Woodward, Bob. 1987. *Veil: The Secret Wars of the CIA, 1981-1987.* New York: Simon and Schuster.

Zimmerman, William. 1984. "Soviet Relations with Yugoslavia and Romania." In *Soviet Policy in Eastern Europe,* edited by Sarah Meiklejohn Terry. New Haven, CT: Yale University Press.

Zirinsky, Michael P. 1994. "The Rise of Reza Khan." In *A Century of Revolution: Social Movements in Iran,* edited by John Foran. Minneapolis: University of Minnesota Press.

About the Author

Mark N. Katz is an Associate Professor of Government and Politics at George Mason University in Fairfax, VA. He received a B.A. in International Relations from the University of California at Riverside in 1976, an M.A. in International Relations from the Johns Hopkins University School of Advanced International Studies in 1978, and a Ph.D. in Political Science from the Massachusetts Institute of Technology in 1982. He has been awarded fellowships and grants by the Brookings Institution, the Earhart Foundation, the Kennan Institute for Advanced Russian Studies, the Rockefeller Foundation, and the United States Institute of Peace.

Katz is also the author of *The Third World in Soviet Military Thought* (1982), *Russia and Arabia: Soviet Foreign Policy toward the Arabian Peninsula* (1986), and *Gorbachev's Military Policy in the Third World* (1989). He has edited two other books and has contributed articles to *The Christian Science Monitor, Current History, International Security, Los Angeles Times, The National Interest, The New York Times, Orbis, Survival, The Wall Street Journal, The Washington Post, The Washington Quarterly,* and other publications.

Index